Frankl's Logotherapy and the Struggle Within

Ajaipal Singh Gill

Ajaipal

Oct. 17, 2000

DORRANCE PUBLISHING CO., INC.
PITTSBURGH, PENNSYLVANIA 15222

ISBN #0-8059-4918-6
Printed in the United States of America

First Printing

For information or to order additional books, please write:
Dorrance Publishing Co., Inc.
643 Smithfield Street
Pittsburgh, Pennsylvania 15222
U.S.A.
1-800-788-7654

To my wife, RAJ,
for her unending support in my life.

Table of Contents

Introduction

Each person's internal striving to discover the mission of his or her life has been the major motivational concern behind the writing of this book. The struggle for this inner search and the daily existential challenges of the Twenty-first century, at times, could be so overwhelming that a person can succumb to a high level of frustration, resulting in feelings of anger, emptiness, and despair. On the contrary, having an understanding of the mission of life could provide a sense of direction that may create the course to steer our life's energies. Since societal living is expected to have potholes, the drive on such a course may not be without obstacles. However, if a person has some grasp of the direction of his or her existence, the strength to encounter those demanding conditions can be dealt with courage.

At the apex of human needs, each of us have a keen desire to actualize our unique individual potentials, and throughout our lifespan we keep on constructing the vertical scaffolding that will eventually enable us to reach the crest of existence. In order to facilitate this challenge, Dr. Viktor E. Frankl, who was a leading psychiatrist of Europe and internationally renowned for his approach to psychotherapy (known as Logotherapy, the Third Viennese School of Psychotherapy), developed a core of concepts that may assist us as a means to the discovery of this meaning of life. The writer has tried to integrate those concepts in the book and has attempted to discuss the ones where he personally had the real-life experience to attest them. As a child, the author has experienced the atrocities of the World War II and has lived during the Japanese occupation of Singapore. Thus, he affirms Dr. Frankl's views. The author himself bears the living evidence of possible human capacities that can serve to surmount life's adversities and transform the sufferings into meaningful ends. Dr. Frankl is a model of survivor and tolerance to the writer and feels highly indebted to him, because even with his very busy life, Dr. Frankl personally took time to guide, review, and edit author's doctoral dissertation. Also, before his death in 1997, he examined and approved the manuscript of this book with the help of his wife.

Dr. Frankl's writings have provided the author with the essential insight to discover the meaning of existence and have offered ideas to manage circumstances that may be extremely distressful into worthy resolves. The writer believes many other individuals struggling to discover the paths of their lives can enhance their internal wisdom and strength by reading this book.

I. The Nature of Person

The realities of life demonstrate that we humans go through life experiences which require a resolve between satisfaction of personal needs and societal demands. To dispense with personal desires in lieu of societal expectations becomes quite an internal struggle. On one hand we are motivated to achieve individual aspirations and on the other the common good. This inner conflict emanates the polarization of one's mental stability and produces tension. Paradoxically the pursuit of personal interests and needs may lead to selfish behaviors and reduction of societal values. Individual actions for personal benefits do emancipate hostility toward others because of disagreements and competition. To strive for a balance between the demands of "self" and the needs of the "others" is on occasions very nerve-racking. At times circumstances are very complex and difficult. However, we as humans do not easily surrender to such pressures blindly and resort to unreasonable responses because our mental structure has the resilience to surmount these complex predicaments. We humans have the capacity to negotiate a balance between these two opposing forces which challenge individual decisions in real life situations. Unfortunately there are living examples that tend to illustrate that some humans have failed to execute this innate capacity and have allowed themselves to be annihilated by situational pressures; and thus, have subjected themselves to aggression and short-term gratifications. Viktor Frankl, who is the founder of *Logotherapy*—today widely known as the "Third Viennese School of Psychotherapy," claims that such acts of personal reduction can be surmounted by finding one's meaning for existence.[1] *Logos* is a Latin word which in English is translated as *meaning*. In Frankl's thinking it is the lack of meaning in life that results into unproductive behaviors. According to Logotherapy, inner balance is feasible because humans have the capacity to think while making judgments in "noetic dimensions."[2] The term *noetic* has been derived from the Greek word "noos" or "nous" which may be translated into English as intellectual or spiritual. This concept of spiritual, in Frankl's thinking, has no theological association.[3] This noetic dimension is the one that offers the humans a sense of direction to resolve the inner tension and struggle and consequentially a harmonious solution. In his theory of Logotherapy, Frankl has further maintained that noetic dimension is free from any form of sickness.[4] Thus, the spiritual dimension enables us to accentuate the inner strengths without any contamination from external pressures. As an extension to this perspective Frankl has also acknowledged in his writings that each person's personality in actuality includes three dimensions; that is, somatic, psychic, and noetic.[5] In accordance to this proposition then, it is understandable

[1] Viktor E. Frankl, *The Will to Meaning: Foundations and Applications of Logotherapy* New York: The World Publishing Company, 1969, p. 63.

[2] Ibid., p. 17.

[3] Viktor E. Frankl, "Religion and Existential Psychotherapy," *Gordon Review*, VI (1960), 2.

[4] Joseph B. Fabry, *The Pursuit of Meaning: Logotherapy Applied to Life*, Boston, Massachusetts: Beacon Press, 1968 p. 25.

[5] Earl A. Grollman, "The Logotherapy of Viktor E. Frankl," *Judaism*, XIV 1965, 27.

that we humans are at risk because of this tri–dimensional division. It is not easy to achieve a happy marriage between the three forces. Integration of these three dimensions does produce a level of stress which is intellectually divisive. The unification of these three dimensions can only be accomplished through qualitative intellectual reasoning. As rational beings we humans are highly responsible creatures and have the ability to avoid selfish temptations. Our responsible and logical assessment of a given situation can lead to productive results. We can exercise our *will* to negate unhealthy thoughts that most likely may generate tension. Based on the principles of logotherapy each person is capable of reasoning in a manner that will lend to positive attitudes and behaviors. If this assumption is correct then, it tends to suggest that the inner dichotomy that is experienced by a person in resolving a contradictory demand can be negotiated by enhancing one's positive attitude. The rebound of an attitude from the negative to the positive is contingent upon human choice and reasoning. But this approach cannot be perceived as that simple and easy. We have to be mindful of the fact that each individual is unique and to some extent has personal limitations, and there are some who claim that the human nature is somewhat irresponsible and selfish (especially in the context of today's materialistic milieu). These conditions can lead to erroneous behaviors. It is not my intention to justify that inappropriate human actions, such as apathy and violence, stem from societal inequities and injustices. If we recognize the fact that each person is unique and possesses different limitations and strengths, then we should have some accommodation for human fallibility too. To strive for a unity when three dimensions are affecting a person's behavioral response simultaneously does become a challenge resulting into inner fracture and tension. Some humans have learned to integrate these three dimensions (somatic, psychic, and noetic) through personal growth and critical thinking, but a few unfortunate ones do fail to arrive at a logical compromise and make mistakes. Besides, in today's society one can find a few who may not consider the need for a healthy compromise and instead may select to simply escape from these tensions by submitting themselves to the use of destructive approaches, for instance, addiction to drugs or physical gratifications. Are these individuals, then, voluntarily surrendering their noetic or spiritual worth?

Facts of living do demonstrate that a few individuals are, in actuality, incapable of entering into these spiritual solutions due to the lack of mental abilities, thus, they choose behavioral responses that are least constructive. This is where society has the responsibility to provide assistance and eventually facilitate constructive judgments and also help the person to realize that in the final analysis an individual is self–determining and has the freedom to take a stand against his circumstances.[6] Life is a challenge and the more we endeavor to encounter this inner conflict the more meaningful our existence becomes. The paths of life are seldom linear and entail a high chance for disappointments and failures. In as much

---

[6] Viktor E. Frankl, *The Will to Meaning: Foundations and Applications of Logotherapy* New York: The World Publishing Company, 1969, p. 16.

as the construction of a road is determined by the physical strata of the land, so we humans should be prepared to make adjustments subject to the demands of time and situations. Any rigid defiance will only lead to further stress and mental imbalance. Recent history provides sufficient examples to prove how timely adaptations have resulted into meaningful outcomes. Just consider for a moment the political changes that have taken place in South Africa, the Soviet Union, and the Middle East. Even in the context of a social change our current perception of the feminine gender being away from home and equal is more meaningful. These examples tend to suggest that an appropriate adjustment corresponding to the demands of the time can create conditions which enhance genuine inner peace and harmony. Keep in mind, I am not recommending an all-out liquidation of individual values and beliefs, but a rational compromise. The spiritual dimension of a person is not designed to promote antagonism and belligerent behavior, nor does it initiate isolation of oneself and the establishment of individual cocoons; instead, it espouses cohesive peaceful living. We are individual islands by nature but stationed within a societal archipelago. To a large extent we are responsible and caring beings and do not expand our destiny at the expense of others, yet it is our personal assessment and attitude towards external circumstances that ultimately makes the significant difference in living. Our cognitive maps can either facilitate an inner peace or create a frame of mind that eventually leads to chaotic living. Just as we have to pay a premium price to obtain a special material object or product, in the same way in order to reduce unnecessary mental distress we have to sacrifice our unreasonable personal expectations and desires. We, at times, have to reorganize our mental sets. Such changes in the end do pay dividends. An individual is capable of separating himself from the past habits and thoughts if they interfere with spiritual gains. We can transcend the egotistic plain and reject yielding to short-term selfish benefits. However, if one does surrender to irrational practices without enlightened deliberations, then he has shifted away from life's real meaning. In the long-term, this type of attitude will be unproductive both for the individual and the society of which he is a part. A lasting sense of inner peace cannot be accrued by submission to selfish personal gains nor by blind adherence to external pressures. In fact, it will produce an inner rebellion and frustration. As individuals we are unique and there is bound to be a diversity in our approaches to seeking inner balance, and these variations become more pronounced when we are living in a society that is educated and capable of making judgments on their own. This kind of behavior is quite obvious in the Western society. These variations are justifiable since they create authentic responses and novel actions. Besides, contradiction is the real tool to evaluate any existing or newer ideas. Group concurrence without any dissension has its fallacies too. We need to work through individual variations by objective and respectful mutual understandings and not by suppression as it happened in the recent history of China (the Tienamen Square). This bridling experience is very frustrating to a creative person and permeates a sense

6

of failure and rejection. Such rejections are pernicious and have the potential to germinate serious revolts, however, human mental make-up has the flexibility to contain and defuse the agony and move on. By nurturing the personal insult or to think of seeking revenge, a person is only depleting his mental energy and stability. This kind of negative attitude will stall creative growth and delay the discovery of one's meaning for existence. Under these perplexing circumstances a person has to make a choice between living in the past (and thus limiting personal growth) or moving forward and facilitating meaningful existence. In my judgment the past should become a springboard to jump forwards, but not a stumbling block, and this is the essence of human mental capacity.

In a global way each individual is a part of the larger world society yet he retains his personal freedom to shape and change the world society by being responsible and optimistic. Humans were responsible in the erection of the Berlin Wall and finally in its destruction. For many years the Wall generated nothing more than frustration and anger, and it did not ideally serve the mankind. Imagine how beautiful it is to live in a world without walls? Such a world will permit humans to develop freely in their own unique way, with least obstruction, and help to profit the most from the entire natural space. Deep in our mind we do have this worldly vision and the desire to move around the surface of the earth freely, yet we are responsible for delineating both physical and mental enclosures. Eventually these barriers, both physical or mental, produce conflicts and insecurities among humans and a mistrust of each other. In this context, logotherapy views a person, "as a being who continuously decides what he is: a being who equally harbors the potential to descend to the level of an animal or to ascend to the life of a saint."[7] To actualize the best of the two will depend on the choice one makes. We are thinking beings and not pre–wired mechanical products or species, we are capable of designing the course of our lives. As rational beings we are capable of emitting the most useful responses, but the selection of a response is contingent upon a person's own values and belief system, as well as honest and firm commitment to those values and beliefs. Each human mind has a filter of its own to evaluate external events. These filters have the capacity to separate impurities that have the risk of limiting human growth. However, these filters do get subjected to external pressures (caused by chemical interventions, such as drugs or material temptations) resulting into personal devastations. The risk for damage is, to some extent, higher in today's society, and daily the media attempts to substantiate this reality. From the documentation of daily events, it appears as if humans are far more vulnerable now than they were in the past decades.

The primary concern of logotherapy is that each individual, under all circumstances, should make every effort to reach the highest level of self–worth and must not be discouraged by the adversities of life. Life is an assignment and it includes complex challenges; therefore, an escape from these pressing

---

[7] Viktor E. Frankl, *Psychotherapy and Existentialism: Selected Papers on Logotherapy* New York: Washington Square Press, Inc., 1967, p. 110.

demands will inhibit the discovery of self–worth and meaning of life. The quality of decisions a person makes, especially during most trying situations, determines the level of one's mental maturity and indirectly the vision of self and the purpose for living. In the final analysis it is the nature of a choice what truly differentiates the cleavage between a person who has a goal for living and the one who is confused about his destination. Humans think, deliberate, and carefully select the alternatives and avoid instinctive resolutions. Besides, hasty judgments do miss the synthesis of possible rational alternatives. In the end constructive and meaningful decisions do promote inner peace and a sense of accomplishment. Even then, because we are humans, there is always the chance of an error or failure but at least one can claim that he or she did make an attempt to find a direction in life, which in itself is a sign of courage and growth. In case of a failure and the honest recognition of it gives a person the opportunity to move on rather than being restricted by the feelings of shame triggered by the failure. In contrast a person who images himself as a perfect being and above mistakes will make his life miserable and stressful. Some people in order to protect this image of perfection at times choose to become defiant and aggressive. It is true that admission of a personal mistake does have risks of its own, but at least it is free from self–deceit and false pride. Denial of personal failures on the other hand will compound the mental anguish and may even limit the opportunity for personal growth and improvement. We see some political leaders of the world doing exactly the same and they attempt to defend their failures of judgment just to support their false sense of self–pride at the expense of the people and the resources of the country amounting to an economic collapse. On the contrary the spiritual nature of an individual is in actuality distanced from such dishonest practices and living.

While speaking of *existence*, Frankl claims that he has used this word to specify that the nature of a person is highly dynamic and it has an "on–going" implication. Frankl has further emphasized that the term "existential" may be used to refer to: (1) existence itself; that is, a specific mode of being; (2) the meaning of existence; that is, the purpose for existence; and (3) the striving to discover this purpose for existence.[8] It is the third point of view that is of particular significance to the principles of logotherapy. Frankl recognizes that this striving to discover the special meaning for existence is expected to produce an inner tension because it offers a real challenge in life.

In logotherapy each person is encouraged to perceive and interpret this phenomenon of inner tension as a responsibility rather than an anguish in life. This inner struggle should not be viewed as a burden nor an imposition by the society, but one's spiritual need and desire. Each person should recognize that this need is an integral part of his or her existence and not an obligation in life. Frankl places the responsibility to discover one's meaning in life on each person and proposes that each individual must make a concerted effort to find what he is and what he is capable of

---

[8] Viktor E. Frankl, "Basic Concepts of Logotherapy," *Journal of Existential Psychiatry*, III (1962-63), 112.

becoming during his existence.[9] Frankl insists that person's main concern in life is not to seek pleasure or to avoid suffering but rather to accomplish an assignment of life which is beyond personal gratifications and satisfactions.[10] Here, one must not think that logotherapy identifies itself with moral teaching. In fact, logotherapy is an open–ended philosophy which can feed into other disciplines without any reference to moralistic perspective. In logotherapy, it is the individual decisions and the selection of personal choices that is at the crux of the theory and not the value judgment of others. After all it is the individual, who in the end has to assume the responsibility for his actions and decisions, and to interpret the significance of his actions in terms of humanity, society, conscience, or God.[11] It is the individual who determines the direction and the purpose for his existence and not the society, and this is the basic premise of logotherapy.

Logotherapy attempts to offer insights into one's inner–self and encourages each person to find the ultimate tasks of existence. It helps the individual to discover his inner strengths and weaknesses and create a vision for the future that will lead to meaningful existence. It helps to understand that intellectual activities alone do not make life meaningful; instead, one should seek something beyond the academic activities. To Frankl it is important to exceed the intellectual pursuits and explore one's spiritual self because it is this spiritual enlightenment that enables a person to

[9] Viktor E. Frankl, *Man's Search for Meaning: An Introduction to Logotherapy* New York: Washington Square Press, Inc., 1963, p. 173.

[10] Ibid., p. 164.

[11] Viktor E. Frankl, *The Will to Meaning: Foundations and Applications of Logotherapy* New York: The world Publishing Company, 1969, p. 143.

discover the ultimate tasks of his existence. Frankl claims that this personal spiritual awakening in the end elevates human existence to much higher levels of living and spares the individual from becoming selfish and indulging in acquiring basic needs and gratifications. An insight into one's spiritual self provides a person with the working relationship and the sense of balance required between the cerebral and the emotional mind. When a person's mind is in an emotional overdrive it is the spiritual self that exercises a spontaneous control and converts the potentially harmful energy into rational outcomes. In logotherapy there is strong emphasis on the need for spirituality and meaningfulness in human thoughts and actions. Logotherapy contains some very valuable concepts and ideas and is based on the following three major concepts: (1) the freedom of will; (2) the will to meaning; and (3) the meaning of life.[12]

Thus, it is appropriate to examine these primary tenets of logotherapy in more detail, and to begin with let me analyze and interpret Frankl's concept of "freedom of will." Frankl firmly believes that every human being does have a choice of action and this option is available under both easy and worst circumstances of life. He writes:

> Man can preserve a vestige of spiritual freedom, of independence of mind, even in such terrible conditions of psychic and physical stress,

---

[12] Viktor E. Frankl, *The Will to Meaning: Foundations and Applications of Logotherapy* New York: The World Publishing Company, 1969, p. vii.

> everything can be taken from a man
> but one thing: the last of the human
> freedoms—to choose one's attitude
> in any given set of circumstances, to
> choose one's own way.[13]

Life experiences do concur with the above assumption and remind us that a person's wealth and material objects are subjected to loss and elimination but not his freedom of will, because this attribute of an individual belongs to his spiritual mind. An individual has the capacity to resist and stand bravely against conditions, however threatening, which encroach upon his freedom of will. Frankl has asserted that, "Man's freedom is no freedom from conditions but rather freedom to take a stand on whatever adverse conditions might confront him."[14] It is this individual freedom that provides the capacity to encounter and manage circumstances that are extremely difficult in one's life. A person retains the freedom to decide whether to acquiesce or confront the demanding challenges of life. According to the principles of logotherapy a person is free to choose a positive or negative attitude toward his past and present conditions. One can even rise above the biological limitations with a proper attitude. In essence, it is the personal psychological frame of mind that can either facilitate the human potentials to a success or freeze the capacities resulting into a disaster. In Frankl's words, "Man is not fully conditioned and determined; he determines himself whether to give in

---

[13] Viktor E. Frankl, *Man's Search for Meaning: An Introduction to Logotherapy.* New York: Washington Square Press, Inc., 1963, p. 104.

[14] Viktor E. Frankl, *The Will to Meaning: Foundations and Applications of Logotherapy.* New York: The World Publishing Company, 1969, p. 16.

to conditions or stand up to them. In other words, man is ultimately self–determining."[15] He further adds that a young person does not have to surrender to unhealthy life styles just because of his conditions of birth and other related unproductive environmental circumstances. The young person can obviously take a stand against his adverse conditions and determine the future course of his life that will eventually counter the unhealthy circumstances of his birth.

Frankl does not refute the fact that environmental and hereditary factors do influence the extent of human freedom, but in themselves those factors never limit the human capacity to take a stand toward such conditions.[16] Thus, it is the individual's attitude that eventually delineates the boundaries of such biological limitations and gives credence to them. Frankl adamantly supports this perspective and has maintained that there is nothing conceivable which would so condition a person as to leave him without the slightest opportunity to exercise his personal freedom.[17]

Frankl is opposed to rigid determinism since it assumes that human actions are influenced by predetermined psychic forces and a person has no liberty at all to decide for himself. Frank argues that the Freudian conception of "psychic–determinism" is incomplete because in it a person is pictured as if he is driven by predetermined unconscious drives and motives; therefore, there is very little that a person

---

[15] Viktor E. Frankl, *Man's Search For Meaning: An Introduction to Logotherapy,* New York: Washington Square Press, Inc., 1963, p. 206.

[16] Victor E. Frankl, "Dynamics, Existence, and Values," *Journal of Existential Psychiatry,* II (1961-62), 6.

[17] Viktor E. Frankl, "Basic Concepts of Logotherapy," *Journal of Existential Psychiatry,* III (1962), 117.

can consciously do to modify his or her past or present circumstances. From a cognitive perspective, it is important to recognize that, it is not the situation which limits the personal freedom; instead, it is the individual's perception of the situation that delineates the limitations. In view of this, a person has the mental capacity to conquer his psychobiological determinants either by confronting them with a positive attitude or by restructuring the mental outlook towards them. In reality, each person is capable of reorganizing his mental make-up towards circumstances that are negative in nature. Without doubt a person is vulnerable to his psychobiological limitations, but at least he can take the initiative to modify the course of his future life by creating a positive frame of mind. Frankl repeatedly affirms this point of view and says that, "Within limits, too, man has more alternatives than he ever realizes. A human being, it is true, is a finite thing. However, to the extent to which he understands his finiteness, he also overcomes it."[18] The real meaning to the complexities of physical environment and events of life, in the end is assigned by our own mental make-up. The physical events and objects provide the basic challenges but the mind eventually offers interpretations to these perplexing predicaments. Such crossroads are not uncommon in real living and can lead to a difficult interplay between the physical event and the mental assessment of the same to a complete stop. The biological structures do provide the blueprint for human capacities but their unfolding for maximum expansion is facilitated by

[18] Viktor E. Frankl, "Psychiatry and Man's Quest for Meaning," *Journal of Religion and Health,* I (1961-62), p. 103.

our personal attitude and fortitude. A person has to courageously work through the physical limits and transform the sharp bends into smooth turns. Human mind has the resilience to surmount the biological or physical barriers and assign new meanings and directions to them. Humans choose the path of action and have a purpose in making intentional decisions. Thus, freedom, for Frankl, means freedom in the face of instinctive forces, inherited personality traits, and environmental inhibitions.[19] Each individual, according to Frankl, must free himself from his unfavorable circumstances in his own unique way; and thus, strive for self-actualization. In logotherapy man is perceived to own the capacity to encounter his challenging situations by mobilizing his inner defiant spirit.[20] This means that, in spite of man's environmental constraints, he still retains the freedom to confront his adverse circumstances. Man's actions are not confined to hereditary and environmental provisions but upon decisions that he makes by engaging his free will. Man has the freedom to modify his past attitudes and understandings and look for new appreciations and meanings. Man is not a permanent mechanical object but a creative and dynamic being. Man cannot be compelled into making choices purely on the basis of circumstances or whatever is available to him. "Man is not driven; man decides," say Frankl.[21] If it rests on a person to decide, then, should the decision be

---

[19] Viktor E. Frankl, "The Concept of Man in Psychotherapy," *Pastoral Psychology* VI (November, 1955), p. 23.

[20] Magda B. Arnold and John A. Gasson, "Logotherapy and Existential Analysis," *The Human Person*, New York: Ronald Press, 1954, p. 483.

[21] Viktor E. Frankl, "Collective Neuroses of the Present Day," *Universitas* IV (1961), p. 311.

devoid of an appropriate meaning and responsibility? Obviously not, because it will result into a destruction of normal life; therefore, freedom must not be separated from responsibility. We are accountable for our decisions and owe an obligation to the society of which we happen to be a part. In this context, Frankl has clearly incorporated the idea of responsibility in the exercise of human freedom. Freedom, says Frankl, degenerates into mere arbitrariness unless it is lived in terms of responsibility.[22] In logotherapy it is assumed that a person is responsible in his thoughts and actions and intends to become the best in each moment of his existence.[23] Contrary to Frankl's view, Jean–Paul Sartre, a noted existentialist, has failed to relate this idea of human responsibility to freedom in his writings.[24] Although both emphasize seeing man as free rather than the product of conditioning, only Frankl has incorporated the idea of responsibility in the expression of human freedom. Frankl does acknowledge that mentally sick people, deterministic philosophers, and persons who intentionally poison their mind are not aware of their freedom.[25] He further states that freedom to some may be denied through illness, disability, or circumstances such as regimented censorship by a political system. Even under these adverse conditions a person is capable of overcoming the

[22] Viktor E. Frankl, *The Will to Meaning: Foundations and Applications of Logotherapy,* New York: The World Publishing Company, 1969, p. 49.

[23] Viktor E. Frankl, "Psychiatry and Man's Quest for Meaning," *Journal of Religion and Health,* I (1061-62), p. 127.

[24] Robert E. Leslie, "Viktor E. Frankl's New Concept of Man," *Motive,* XXII (March 1962), p. 17.

[25] Viktor E. Frankl, *Psychotherapy and Existentialism: Selected Papers on Logotherapy* New York: Washington Square Press, Inc., 1967, p. 2.

limitations by healthy imaginations, personal courage, and by enhancing one's level of tolerance. Frankl says, "Man has the capacity to detach himself from the worst conditions of life by being mentally strong."[26] He has also emphasized that if a person attempts to escape into obscurity from the demands of life, then, the challenges of life remain unresolved and it reflects a degree of irresponsibility on the part of a person. As a matter of fact there are some feeble-minded individuals who choose to escape from the demands of life by resorting to drugs or other irresponsible actions, but such decisions only compound their hardships.

A person by exercising his freedom selects an option between surrendering to an adverse condition or to confront it with personal courage and dignity. The possibility of submitting to difficult circumstances is conceivable because of personal insecurities, lack of knowledge, and limited resources. Besides, there is the fear of failure and being stranded alone, and at times not mentally prepared to encounter the repercussions for being different and defiant. Moreover, a persons' past experience, too, plays an important role in influencing his thought processes and behavior especially when it is diverse and deviates from the mainstream or historical traditions. These thoughts could be counter productive and therefore require an honest assessment when exercising personal freedom. This is where a support from a person's social network can make a meaningful contribution to save him from yielding to obstacles

---

[26] Viktor E. Frankl, *The Will to Meaning: Foundations and Applications of Logotherapy* New York: The World Publishing Company, 1969, p. 16.

and reducing to the mental paradigm of hopelessness or self–destruction. In view of this expectation, logotherapy is certainly helpful and offers insights that can mitigate pessimistic outlooks toward the pressing demands of life.

Looking at the realities of life, man most often is afraid to take a stand and be different because in order to be diverse he has to bear the consequences of his unique actions. Such a feeling of despair is reasonably pervasive among humans, and thus individuals end up yielding to the adverse conditions of life and consequently surrender their freedom of will. Frankl is opposed to this type of attitude since it destroys individual uniqueness and distinction. He further believes that once a man submerges himself into the conditions of his life, it is almost impossible to get out of them.[27] Frankl does not wish to see man becoming an insignificant number in the total crowd, and he firmly believes in individual's capacity to become a unique person. Frankl has an appreciation for individuals who have the courage to take a stand against their circumstance in a creative and responsible manner. A free person, in Frankl's opinion, is one who has acquired the capacity to govern his own destiny, is not dictated to by others like a mechanical object, and he also resents one's blind submission to the misfortunes of life. Frankl says, "Man is by no means merely a product of heredity and environment. There is a third element: decision. Man ultimately decides for himself."[28] This implies

---

[27] Earl A. Grollman, "Viktor E. Frankl: A Bridge Between Psychiatry and Religion," *Conservative Judaism*, XIX (Fall, 1964), p. 21.

[28] Viktor E. Frankl, *The Doctor and the Soul: From Psychotherapy to Logotherapy* New York: (Alfred A. Knopf, Inc., 1965) p. xix.

that man does not simply exist but is continuously deciding for his future existence. Again Frankl claims that through his freedom of will, man is not only able to detach himself from the world but also is capable of self–detachment.[29] This suggests that a person has the capacity to distance himself from his emotions and rise above the negative feelings by being creative and objective. A person is capable of rejecting the subjection of his freedom of will to the demands of the masses through creative imagination and self–determination.

Frankl is against the subjection of human *free will* to collective decisions because it depersonalizes the human being.[30] He is also opposed to considering human beings in terms of a psychic mechanism governed by the law of cause and effect. He asserts that man is not an association of reflexes; in fact, he is inherently self–determining.[31]

As humans we fully realize that life is a continuous stream of change, and like a river, its course is always in the process of change. Just as changes in the course of a river are contingent upon its capacity to erode, similarly the changes in life are dependent upon one's capacity to brave the conditions of living. Like a stream, in order to change its course it has to weather down the physical surroundings in order to acquire a new direction, in the same fashion a person has to confront and modify his environmental conditions to seek new meanings and understandings.

---

[29] Viktor E. Frankl, *Psychotherapy and Existentialism: Selected Papers on Logotherapy* (New York: Alfred A. Knopf, Inc., 1967), p. 28.

[30] Viktor E. Frankl, "Dynamics, Existence, and Values," *Journal of Existential Psychiatry*, II (1961-62), p. 8.

[31] Ibid.

Changes in the human mind most often take place by braving the conditions of life and not by submitting to them. For Frankl opting to take a stand toward the conditions of life means exerting freedom.

Each day man experiences some moments of life which are difficult to resolve and from which there is no escape, thus he is compelled to make rational decisions about them. Such predicaments do provide opportunities for new insights and learnings and in a way personal growth. The likelihood of human mental growth sometimes depends on such challenging moments. Under such trying periods one has to make decisions that are not erroneous but sensible because these decisions implicate the worth and the caliber of a person. The quality of decisions made under stress are very unfolding and speak a lot about a person's hidden personality. As Frankl has remarked, "Man possesses the potentialities to be a saint or a beast, which one of these actualizes depends upon his decisions but not on conditions."[32]

It is very crucial to deliberate and think before one makes a decision because at times it is hard to change one's decision; therefore one must select the available alternative with serious considerations. The constraints of society, too, limit our freedom to alter the decision, and under circumstances one has to be prepared to face the consequences of wrong actions. "What man has done, cannot be undone. Whereas he is responsible for what he has done; he is not free to undo it."[33]   However Frankl does believe that man

---

[32] Viktor E. Frankl, "Angel as Much as Beast," *Unitarian Universalist Register–Leader*, CXLIV (February, 1963), p. 9.

[33] Viktor E. Frankl, "Existential Escapism," *Motive* XXIV (January–February, 1964), p. 12.

has the capacity to free himself from the anxieties of his past decisions that were apparently wrong and inappropriate by surmounting his personal sense of guilt. We don't have to live in the past; instead the past should be perceived as a springboard to jump forwards and move on.

In his writings Frankl has also addressed the issue of human freedom and life's moral demands. In real life moral demands can pose a head–on collision with our personal desires and may lend to create serious challenges. Encountering such conflicts may not be simple and could require a very thoughtful search, but as rational beings we are capable of accentuating our moral strengths and sail through such moral dilemmas with productive and meaningful judgments. We are guided by our spirituality and assume full responsibility for our decisions and actions. We most often tend to avoid judgments leading to self–destruction and moral indignity. We can attempt to visualize the consequences of our actions and thus make an effort to stay away from choices that are immoral. Frankl has emphasized that, "man is never driven to moral behavior; in each instance he decides to behave morally. He does so for the sake of a cause to which he commits himself."[34]

This quality of a person may be interpreted to mean that each person is guided by his own meaning of life which includes a value system and spirituality. Absence of this ethical structure may result into lack of moral fiber in man so vital to make meaningful judgments.

---

[34] Viktor E. Frankl, *Man's Search for Meaning: An Introduction to Logotherapy* (New York: Washington Square Press, Inc., 1963), p. 158.

Thus, man is free, and he is what he makes of himself. Man has the capacity to rise above his conditions however stressful they might be. In Frankl's words, "Man can preserve a vestige of spiritual freedom, of independence of mind, even in such terrible conditions of psychic and physical stress."[35] There are times in life when one is in complex dilemmatic conditions but is expected to make a decision. It requires courage and a balanced mind. Yielding to such circumstances will be an easy way out but it entails compromising one's personal freedom of will. This is exactly what Frankl is opposed to because he claims that regardless of the individual's condition, each person has the freedom to influence and modify the circumstances of his life.

---

[35] *Ibid.*, p. 104.

II. Will to Meaning

The "will to meaning" represents an effort on the part of an individual to find a purpose for one's existence. One of the tenets of logotherapy assumes that man is continuously struggling to discover his life's mission which will ultimately guide his thoughts and actions during the discourse of living. Frankl believes that each person has a specific purpose or cause for which he lives and struggles in life. This specific purpose or cause serves as the primary force in our behavioral pursuits. This inner force, namely the *will to meaning*, has been defined by Frankl in these words:

> What I call the will to meaning could be defined as the basic striving of man to find and fulfill meaning and purpose.[36]

This definition asserts that the basic motivational force in man's life is the striving to discover a meaning for his existence. Frankl also explains that man alone is gifted with this capacity and the initiative to discover the meaning for life, whereas the lower species do not possess this ability. He says, "Will to meaning is the most human phenomenon of all, since an animal certainly never worries about the meaning of its existence."[37] This may be translated to mean that Frankl is suggesting to man that he has a unique capacity to distinguish himself from the lower organisms by first

---

[36] Viktor E. Frank, *The Will to Meaning: Foundations and Applications of Logotherapy* New York: The World Publishing Company, 1969), p. 35.

[37] Viktor E. Frankl, *The Doctor and the Soul: From Psychotherapy to Logotherapy* (New York: Alfred A. Knopf, Inc. 1965), p. x.

discovering and then accomplishing tasks which are worthwhile and make a significant difference in life. In Frankl's views man is not solely interested in driving himself to satisfy the basic organismic needs but:

> Man's search for meaning is a primary force in his life and not a secondary rationalization of instinctual drives.[38]

Frankl did not speak of the will to meaning in terms of biological homeostasis or the realization of material gratifications but, instead, something higher than the basic needs. Furthermore, Frankl has drawn a distinction between being driven to something and striving for something by explaining that the connotation behind the word drive leads one to perceive that the person is pushed into reaching a goal whereas the word striving has an implicit understanding of being pulled toward a destination (meaning of life).[39]

Thus, Frankl prefers to see man striving for some meaningful objective in life rather than being driven to the reduction of some personal physical demand. To discover the meaning of existence is a spiritual necessity and not an encroachment on one's biological makeup. This basic *will* is not a personal trait or an instinctive disposition, but an understanding of some specific goal in life; that is, the essence of one's existence. Some writers think that the will to meaning has

---

[38] Viktor E. Frankl, *Man's Search for Meaning: An Introduction to Logotherapy* (New York: Washington Square Press, Inc., 1963), p. 154.

[39] Viktor E. Frankl, "Self-Transcendence as a Human Phenomenon," *Journal of Humanistic Psychology*, VI (Fall, 1966), p. 100.

an ontological and cosmological implications,[40] but Frankl has distanced himself from such interpretations and has limited the concept of *will* to striving for a purpose in life and its meaningful fulfillment. Frankl maintains that man is a purposive organism and the activation of his mental energy is always directed toward accomplishing some meaningful end. A person has the capacity to organize insights that will lead into the discovery of one's worth, and to eventuate such a meaningful closure becomes a challenge, and it requires a serious struggle in life. In view of this Frankl has emphasized that the meaning of life cannot be assigned to a person, but can only be found through self–discovery. On the other hand, Frankl's conception of the *will to meaning* is distinctly different from Freud's "pleasure principle" or Adler's "will to power," which is depicted in the following writings:

> ...the will to power on one hand, and the pleasure principle, on the other hand, are derivations of man's primary concern, ... Only if one's original concern with meaning fulfillment is frustrated is one either content with power or intent on pleasure. Both happiness and success are mere substitutes for fulfillment...[41]

[40] James C. Crumbaugh and Leonard T. Maholick, "The Case for Frankl's Will to Meaning," *Journal of Existential Psychiatry*, XIV (1963), p. 43.

[41] Viktor E. Frankl, *The Will to Meaning: Foundations and Applications of Logotherapy* (New York: The World Publishing Company, 1969), p. 35.

This shows that Frankl is not only admonishing those individuals who just care for seeking pleasure or acquisition of the material power in their lives, but he is also making them aware of their short–sightedness in perceiving the purpose for their existence. According to Frankl, pleasure, happiness, or power is never the ultimate goal of human striving; in fact, it is representative of a failure to find the real purpose for existence.[42] In Frankl's words if a person makes happiness the primary objective of his motivation, then he loses sight of the ultimate reason for existence.

In contrast to Freud's drive–reduction principle, Frankl has proposed a meaning–seeking principle in which he assumes that man's efforts are not directed toward the gratification of basic needs and physical pleasure, but toward some specific tasks which are worthy of oneself. Frankl asserts that pleasure is normally not an aim of human motivation but an effect of the achievement of a worthwhile task.[43] In other words, pleasure is automatically accomplished the moment one has fulfilled a worthwhile cause. Thus pleasure is never the primary concern of man's drive and behavior in logotherapy. Frankl further affirms that, "If a man really attempted to gain pleasure by making it his target, he would necessarily fail, for he would miss what he had aimed at."[44] Paul Tillich, too, made a statement quite consistent to this view of Frankl, and said:

---

[42] *Ibid*, p. 34.
[43] Viktor E. Frankl, *Psychotherapy and Existentialism: Selected Papers on Logotherapy* (New York: Washington Square Press, Inc., 1967), p. 40.
[44] *Ibid*.

To seek pleasure for the sake of pleasure is to avoid reality, the reality of other beings and the reality of ourselves. But only the fulfillment of what we really are can give us joy.[45]

In Frankl's views a pleasure–seeking person is obviously frustrated in life and he has illustrated his thoughts on pleasure in these words accrued from his own life experiences:

> ... If any of my ... books has become a success it has been that book [*Man's Search for Meaning*] which I initially planned to publish anonymously ... that book which I wrote under the conviction that it would not, ... bring in success ... actually became a success ... Success and happiness must happen, and the less one cares for them, the more they can.[46]

To Frankl the pleasure principle is self–defeating and must not be considered as the major objective of one's life. In his contention, a person must accomplish some worthwhile goal in order to attain authentic and permanent happiness in life. The fulfillment of a meaningful goal will eventually bring forth real happiness and pleasure in one's life.

---

[45] Paul Tillich, *The New Being* (New York: Charles Scribner's Sons, 1955), p. 146.

[46] Viktor E. Frankl, *The Will to Meaning: Foundations and Applications of Logotherapy* (New York: The World Publishing Company, 1969), p. 35.

Frankl claims that Freud has associated human motives with some underlying forces, but he (Freud) never took human phenomenon at its face value.[47] Frankl is opposed to the idea of reducing human motives merely to repressed drives and instincts; instead he sees a purpose and meaning in human strivings and endeavors. Frankl says that Freud has overlooked the fundamental fact which lends itself to a phenomenological analysis; that is human *will* to reach out for an ultimate meaning in life.[48] Frankl sees man's strivings explicitly in terms of a *will* and not as unconscious hidden energy behind or beneath human motives—as it is viewed in the Freudian psycho-analysis. Freud has not taken into account human drives which willingly tend to seek goals that have significance for a person beyond one's self and personal pleasure.

While speaking of the Adlerian conception of human striving, Frankl says that it too is inadequate in its explanation about human motives. According to Frankl, The Adlerian psychologists assume that the primary cause for human motives is the desire to acquire a certain degree of power and status in the nexus of society. Frankl has attributed this intent of empowering oneself as another form of drive–reduction principle and he asserts that the Adlerian explanation for human motivation is also incomplete because it refers the human drive to gaining inner equilibrium or fulfilling the deficiency. He emphasizes that man can never gain power or status by directly aiming at it. Frankl claims that at a higher

[47] Viktor E. Frankl, *Psychologotherapy and Existentialism: Selected Papers on Logotherapy* (New York: Washington Square Press, Inc., (1967), p. 7.
[48] *Ibid.*

level human strivings do not operate on the means–end principle,[49] and also nor can human activation be viewed as mechanical conditioning—rather it is an intentional effort to achieve something more significant.

Frankl believes that the Freudian "pleasure principle" and the Adlerian "will to power" inadequately describe the purpose of human endeavors.[50] Frankl's contention is that human beings are motivated to find a meaning in life and not the gratification of basic needs. Thus, in logotherapy, the Epicurean happiness (or the *bon vivant*) is not assumed to be the primary focus of human motivation, and neither it is the stoic rejection of such needs the main goal; instead, the emphasis is on reaching for a worthwhile cause. This confirms the philosophical belief that we humans acquire the basics of life in order to reach out to a much higher end, and the final destination is far superior than the daily ordinary benefits and until that goal remains deficient humans keep on striving.

In congruence with this criticism, Frankl has extended his dissatisfaction with Erich Fromm's explanation about human motivation as well. In order to authenticate his criticism, Frankl has referred to one of Fromm's books, titled *Beyond the Chains of Illusion*, in which Fromm speaks of the human motivating forces in terms of drives.[51] This is unacceptable to Frankl because he thinks that man is not driven in life but is continuously striving to discover the purpose of

---

[49] *Ibid.*, p. 39.

[50] Viktor E. Frankl, "The Will to Meaning, *Christian Century,* LXXXI (April 22, 1964), 515.

[51] Erich Fromm, *Beyond The Chains Of Illusion*, (New York: Simon and Schuster, Inc., 1962), p. 38.

his life. Frankl further emphasizes that man is not primarily concerned with the restoration of his physiological imbalance but rather with the discovery of his real purpose in living. Frankl has an intense dislike for interpretations that equate human effort to nothing more than the basic drive to materialize primary needs. By the same token Frankl has expressed concerns about Carl G. Jung's "analytical psychology," too. Frankl asserts that in his analytical psychology, Jung has also portrayed and interpreted man's behavioral pursuits in terms of drives and urges.[52] In the perspective of Jungian psychology, a person is basically driven to the materialization of his or her unconscious desires and urges, but this is not true in the context of logotherapy. Frankl resents the idea of reducing human strivings to the level of nothing beyond getting rid of unpleasant desires or the gratification and the materialization of biological needs and unconscious urges. Frankl says that the Freudian, the Adlerian, and the Jungian conceptions of human *will* are missing:

> ... the fundamental fact that man is a being who ... reaches out for meanings to fulfill. This is why I speak of a will to meaning rather than a need for a drive toward meaning. If man were really driven to meaning he would embark on meaning fulfillment solely to rid himself of this drive in order that homeostasis

52 Viktor E. Frankl, *Psychotherapy and Existentialism: Selected Papers on Logotherapy* (New York: Washington Square Press, Inc. 1967), p. 7.

might be restored; at the same time he would no longer be really concerned with meaning but rather with his own equilibrium and thus with himself.[53]

Frankl's stand clearly indicates that man is primarily striving to discover a purpose for his life which is worthy of oneself, and not an inner equilibrium or the reduction of simple needs. The gratification of mundane demands does not fulfill the spiritual vacuum, and nor can the actualization of one's self be achieved by the sheer accomplishment of day–to–day needs, it is something beyond and exceeds our biological makeup. The lack of this discovery of self–worth is obviously symptomatic of several ills in our society today (this point of contention will be addressed at some length later on). As we advance through various stages of our lives, this demand to discover self–worth becomes stronger and the mere realization of deficiency needs gets less important. The glamour to acquire material things begins to weaken, and at times we even perceive the collection of objects as a source of burden and pain. The core of human striving is directed toward the search for a worthy cause in life and not the accumulation of temporary gains. The desire for achieving personal status in society or the gratification of tissue needs may offer limited satisfaction but seriously fail to transcend our lives to a more meaningful stature. The struggle within each person is to ascend to a level which is higher than

---

[53] Viktor E. Frankl, "The Will to Meaning," *Christian Century,* LXXXI (April 22, 1964), 515.

the basics of life and until that stage is discovered a person is bound to experience an intense degree of frustration and, as a result, resorts to seeking satisfaction through primary needs and personal empowerment.

Frankl's conceptual disagreement is not limited to Freud, Adler, Jung, and Fromm but he also finds contradictions with Erik H. Erickson's concept of *identity*.[54] Erikson claims that a person is most often motivated to find a personal identity and goes through critical turmoils in life because of his or her failure to discover this personal station. The lack of this individual identity then leads to personal chaos and eventuates abrupt turns in life, and at times these turns are so sharp that they terminate into self–destruction, alienation, and total confusion. This intense pressure to discover one's personal identity can be very challenging because it is not a thing that is readily available, it is a process and is subject to self–growth. Frankl maintains that man does not struggle for a personal identity in a direct way, but rather finds his identity to the extent to which he commits himself to a *cause* that is detached from one's very personal self.[55] In Frankl's words a person can realize his personal identity by committing himself to a *cause* which is greater than oneself and not simply by making it the direct goal of his intentions. In other words, one can find his personal identity through some specific act of creativity leading to worthwhile accomplishments. Thus, man cannot discover his personal identity by deliberate calculations or by directly aiming

[54] Erik H. Erikson, *Identity, Youth, and Crisis* (New York: W.W. Norton and Company, Inc., 1968), pp. 15-16.

[55] Viktor E. Frankl, *Psychotherapy and Existentialism: Selected Papers on Logotherapy* (New York: Washington Square Press, Inc., 1967), p. 9.

one's effort to a finishing end. The discovery of personal identity or the meaning of one's existence is an ongoing effort culminating into a worthwhile cause. Personal identity, then, is an integral part of that meaningful cause and not an end in itself. In the context of logotherapy, one's personal identity is certainly realized the moment one discovers his life's mission and makes a concerted effort to fulfill it. According to Frankl, this ultimate goal of life is accessible through an act of commitment, which emerges out of the depth of man's personality and is rooted in his total existence.[56] To substantiate this view, Frankl has quoted one of Karl Jasper's statements: "What man is he ultimately becomes through the cause which he has made his own."[57] It is implicit then that the cause or mission of life for which each individual strives will in itself reveal self-realization or personal identity. Abraham H. Maslow, a strong proponent of "self-actualization," agrees with Frankl that self-realization is best achieved via a commitment to an important task or goal in life.[58] Correspondingly, speaking of self-actualization, Frankl says, "Self-actualization is an effect and cannot be the object of intention."[59] Thus, according to Frankl, self-actualization is a by-product of meaning fulfillment—that is to say, it is the side effect of accomplishing worthwhile tasks in life.

[56] Viktor E. Frankl, "Logotherapy and the Challenge of Suffering," *Pastoral Psychology,* XIII (June, 1962), p. 27.

[57] Viktor E. Frankl, "The Will To Meaning," *Christian Century,* LXXXI (April 22, 1964), 516.

[58] Viktor E. Frankl, *The Will to Meaning: Foundations and Applications of Logotherapy* (New York: The World Publishing Company, 1969), p. 38.

[59] Viktor E. Frankl, "Logotherapy and the Challenge of Suffering," *Pastoral Psychology,* XIII (June, 1962), 26.

The term "self-actualization" was first used by Kurt Goldstein in *The Organism*, but later Abraham H. Maslow incorporated it in his theory of motivation (in the book *Motivation and Personality*). The term self-actualization, in Maslow's book, refers to man's intention for self-fulfillment or his desire for actualizing his potentialities.[60] In contrast Frankl says that self-actualization is contravened when deliberately sought after or made an end in itself.[61] Frankl further argues that developing one's set of potentialities is not the primary aim of life either. In general man is not interested in actualizing everything that he is capable of becoming. Frankl has elaborated this point of view by recalling the example of Socrates, who confessed that he (Socrates) had within himself the potentiality to become a criminal, but he had decided to turn away from materializing this potentiality.[62] Frankl further maintains that if self-actualization is made an end in itself and aimed at as the objective of a primary intention, it could not be attained at all,[63] thus, self-actualization is not the ultimate objective of human motivation. Frankl sees a transcendental quality in self-actualization and does not perceive it as an end in itself. According to him, actualization of the organismic needs does not lead into achieving self-realization. Frankl emphasizes that the potentialities of man must be accounted for in the light of meanings and values.[64] The

---

[60] Abraham H. Maslow, *Motivation and Personality* (New York: Harper and Brothers Publishers, 1954) p. 91.

[61] Viktor E. Frankl, "The Will to Meaning," *Christian Century,* LXXXI (April 22, 1964), p. 516.

[62] Viktor E. Frankl, *Psychotherapy and Existentialism: Selected Papers on Logotherapy* (New York: Washington Square Press, Inc., 1967), p. 9.

[63] Viktor E. Frankl, "Logotherapy and the Challenge of Suffering," *Pastoral Psychology,* XIII (June, 1962), 26.

[64] *Ibid.*

purpose of self–actualization cannot be interpreted to mean the fulfillment of subjective goals and nor does it signify the total facilitation of every individual potentialities.

In Frankl's thinking, self–actualization is directed to the realization of some responsible and worthwhile qualities of a person otherwise this effort is futile and vain. In this regard, Maslow is in complete agreement with Frankl and affirms that those persons who seek self–actualization directly and selfishly have very little hope of achieving it.[65] The intent of self–actualization is not geared towards achieving self–centered ends but to a higher destination that will elevate a person to some degree of transcendence. In Frankl's view a person who is bent on actualizing his potentialities without reference to any specific ultimate goal will experience a sense of futility and meaninglessness in his life, which will eventually lead to an *existential frustration*.[66] In reality such a person has failed to understand the specific purpose for his existence, and he further explains that the existential frustration could appear under various masks and guises in life.[67] Frankl explains that a person who experiences meaninglessness in his life has a tendency to compensate the lack of purpose in life by indulging in sexual adventures, hedonistic attitudes, or by escaping into the world of drugs. Frankl has cautioned that existential frustration, however, must not be thought of as a mental disease and says:

---

[65] Abraham H. Maslow, "Comments on Dr. Frankl's Paper," *Journal of Humanistic Psychology,* VI (Fall, 1966), p. 108.

[66] Viktor E. Frankl, *The Will to Meaning: Foundations and Applications of Logotherapy,* (New York: The World Publishing Company, 1969), p. 64.

[67] Viktor E. Frankl, *Man's Search for Meaning: An Introduction to Logotherapy,* (New York: Washington Square Press Inc., 1963), p. 170.

> ... the will to meaning represents not only the most human phenomenon possible, but also that its frustration does not necessarily signify some-thing pathological [involving disease]. A person is not necessarily sick if he thinks that his existence is meaning-less. ... Existential frustration ... is not something pathological [disease–pro-ducing] ... when it is actually patho-genic—that is to say, when it leads to a neurotic illness—such a neurosis is called noogenic neurosis.[68]

It has been explained earlier that *noogenic neurosis* drives from the word *noetic*, and Frankl has used it to represent the spiritual core of man's personality.[69] It refers to the problems of mind and have no religious connotation.[70] The term *noetic* has been literally derived from the Greek word *noos* or *nous*, and is translated in English to mean mind, intellect, or per-ception; therefore in the context of logotherapy it denotes anything that is related to the higher domain of a person. Frankl says that issues such as man's aspiration for a meaningful existence, as well as the frustration of this aspiration, are dealt with by logotherapy in spiritual terms.[71] Speaking of the etiol-ogy of noogenic neuroses, one may find that in

[68] Viktor E. Frankl, "The Will to Meaning," *Journal of Pastoral Care,* XII (1958), 85.

[69] Viktor E. Frankl, *The Will to Meaning: Foundations and Applications of Logotherapy* (New York: The World Publishing Company, 1969), p. 22.

[70] Viktor E. Frankl, *Man's Search for Meaning: An Introduction to Logotherapy* (New York: Washington Square Press, Inc., 1963), p. 159.

[71] *Ibid.*, p. 160.

logotherapy Frankl has assumed the following major cause for it:

> ... Noogenic neuroses do not emerge from conflicts between drives and instincts but rather from conflicts between various values; ... to speak in a more general way, from spiritual problems.[72]

This assumption clearly opposes the Freudian psychology because Freud refers the frustration of the mind to the repressed sexual and aggressive needs of a person, whereas this is not the case in logotherapy. Instead it is the effect of failure to seek a purpose for one's existence that leads into mental or spiritual frustration. Frankl claims that it is the deficiency or lack of this spiritual purpose that has turned individuals in today's society to become very mechanical in their behaviors.[73] Life for some has become a mechanical routine and much of their mechanical energy is limited to achieving basic needs. Because of their mechanical lifestyle they end into a state of confusion and suffer from a sense of meaninglessness in life. They eventually experience intense unhappiness and frustration due to the lack of an understanding of this specific purpose for living. Frankl has attributed a special term to describe this state of inner emptiness, namely, the *existential vacuum*.[74] When a person has failed to

---

[72] *Ibid.*

[73] R.H. Turner, "Comment on Dr. Frankl's Paper," *Journal of Existential Psychiatry,* I (1960), 22.

[74] Viktor E. Frankl, *Man's Search for Meaning: An Introduction to Logotherapy* (New York: Washington Square Press, Inc., 1963), p. 167.

relate his existence to some ultimate goal life does become meaningless. However, Frankl has been prudent in explaining the effects of existential vacuum and has suggested that it should not be correlated to a mental disease. Speaking about the lack of this ultimate purpose Frankl says:

> First, in contrast to an animal, no drives and instincts tell man what he must do. Second, in contrast to former times, no conventions, traditions and values tell him what he should do. Soon, one may predict, he will not even know what he basically wishes to do.[75]

This may be translated to mean that today a person is no longer guided by the traditional customs and values and is also experiencing the problem of futility in life. The symptoms of meaninglessness are very widespread today. Frankl further claims that a youth in the American culture is simply not sure of his or her primary purpose for life and is desperately trying to seek a sense of direction and meaning. Some adults, too, are confused and frustrated in life because they are not aware of their life's mission. Erik H. Erikson has also referred to this pervasive crisis in modern living.[76] One observes a general lack of direction and zeal, especially in youth, and they appear to meander in life like confused wanderers. Frankl assumes that this is

---

[75] Viktor E. Frankl, "Logotherapy," *The Israel Annals of Psychiatry and Related Disciplines,* V (1967), 143.

[76] Erik H. Erikson, *Identity and the Life Cyclel* (New York: International Universities Press, Inc., 1959), p. 91.

due to boredom and apathy, which are the main man-ifestations of existential vacuum.[77] Elaborating on the subject of boredom, Frankl says that this is the effect of mechanical automation as it has increased one's leisure hours, and one really does not know what to do with the excess of free time.[78] With the advent of "high-tech" this has been compounded even more and there is an augmentation of automated alterna-tives. Living is almost directed to the acquisition of material gains, and there is an active promotion of con-spicuous mechanical consumption in terms of here-and-now. Correspondingly to commensurate such a lopsided emphasis very little challenge is offered to the young to discover the ultimate purpose for life, and it is essential in order to maintain a well-balanced living. A meaningful understanding and discovery of life's mission can help to alleviate some of the existential anxieties of a person, and thus, facilitate true self-realization.

The author has now reached to the third basic concept of logotherapy, and that is, the "meaning of life," and plans to examine it in more detail ahead.

---

[77] Viktor E. Frankl, *The Will to Meaning: Foundations and Applications of Logotherapy* (New York: The World Publishing Company, 1969), p. 85.

[78] Viktor E. Frankl, *Man's Search for Meaning: An Introduction to Logotherapy* (New York: Washington Square Press, Inc., 1963), p. 169.

III. Meaning of Life

Frankl was practically forced to confront the question of life's meaning because of his personal experiences as an inmate of Nazi concentration camps and also due to the problems he faced in the daily lives of his patients as a psychiatrist. These factors have influenced him to assume the meaning of life as one of the major tenets of logotherapy. In this connection Frankl has expressed:

> Day by day I am confronted with people ... I am besieged by their cry for an answer to the question of an ultimate meaning to suffering.
>
> I myself went through this purgatory when I found myself in a concentration camp and lost the manuscript of the first version of my first book. Later, ... I asked myself what my life had been for. ... But after wrestling with my despair for hours, ... I finally asked myself what sort of meaning could depend on whether or not a manuscript of mine is printed. ... But if there is meaning, it is unconditional meaning, and neither suffering nor dying can detract from it.[79]

It is obvious from the above that Frankl's own life acquired meaning when the manuscript of his first

---

[79] Viktor E. Frankl, *The Will to Meaning: Foundations and Applications of Logotherapy* (New York: The World Publishing Company, 1969), pp. 155-56.

41

book, *The Doctor and the Soul: An Introduction to Logotherapy*,[80] was confiscated. The will to accomplish this task of writing anew helped him to survive the atrocities of the Nazi concentration camps. It gave him the reason and the specific purpose waiting to be fulfilled. Under the influence of those unfortunate circumstances, he discovered the meaning of his life. Frankl's experiences have led him to believe that the most basic human problem today is this concern for finding the meaning of life. However, its discovery is quite accidental and most often grows out of the situational challenges. In view of this Frankl has remarked that it is futile to predetermine one's life tasks and he has analogically explained that just as in a chess game one cannot plan all the moves in advance, so is the meaning of life.[81] Besides the world in which we are living today is highly mobile and subject to abrupt changes. At times our circumstances can drastically change in a few seconds. In Frankl's thinking life's real circumstances are the ones that eventually determine the true meaning and not any kind of predetermination.[82]

This concern for finding the meaning of one's life is not new among thinkers; even Rene Descartes (1596–1650), a French philosopher and mathematician, was interested in this human phenomenon. However, the solution to this problem is not easy and over the years (especially nowadays) has become more complicated. Comparatively in the past, life was simpler, and man maintained a higher degree of unity

---

[80] Viktor E. Frankl, *Man's search for Meaning: An Introduction to Logotherapy* (New York: Washington Square Press, Inc., 1963), p. 165.

[81] *Ibid.*, p. 172

[82] *Ibid.*, p. 171.

with the nature. The momentum, expectations, and pressures of life are very different today. Frankl has attempted to resolve the problem of the meaning of life by suggesting that it is inappropriate to seek an answer to this question by directly asking a person: "What is the meaning of life?" Frankl says:

> ... man should not ask what he may expect from life, but should rather understand that life expects something from him. It may also be put this way: in the last resort, man should not ask "what is the meaning of my life?" but should realize that he himself is being questioned. Life is putting its problems to him, and it is up to him to respond to these questions by being responsible; he can only answer to life by answering for his life.[83]

The above statement implies that one must not expect something from life; instead, one should question oneself: What must I do in order to make my life more meaningful and worthwhile? From Frankl's point of view, life is an opportunity to accomplish some worthwhile tasks and he has emphasized that there is meaning in every existence and the decision to find that meaning depends on an individual. It is the individual who in the end assigns a meaning to his or her own life and such encounters are experienced during trying times and challenging conditions. One

---

[83] Viktor E. Frankl, *The Doctor and the Soul: From Psychotherapy to Logotherapy* (New York: Alfred A. Knopf, Inc., 1965) p. xv.

cannot discover the meaning of life by placing pleasure or power as pivotal in one's existence. In this context, Frankl says:

> When we set up pleasure as the whole meaning of life, we insure that in the final analysis life shall inevitably seem meaningless. Pleasure cannot possibly lend meaning to life.[84]

Life's meaning, then, is not contingent upon the acquisition of material wealth or in the gratification of pleasurable motives. In Frankl's judgment, the question of life's meaning is evaded by people who anchor their thoughts to pleasure or power as the primary aspiration of life. In other words, persons who resort to sexual satisfactions and intoxicating pleasures are without directions and are escaping from the responsibility of finding the meaning of their existence. Such individuals are somewhat lost and defeated in their purpose for living. Frankl is of the opinion that persons who claim that their lives are meaningless, or have no meaning other than seeking pleasure, are not conscious of their capacities which can lead them to some worthy destination. In fact to support his point of view, Frankl has quoted Albert Einstein: "The man who regards his life as meaningless is not merely unhappy but is hardly fit for life."[85] Life always has a meaning and no human challenge or condition is without a meaning. The meaning of life can never be arbitrarily assigned to a person; he has to

---

[84] *Ibid.,* p. 37.

[85] Viktor E. Frankl, *The Will to Meaning: Foundations and Applications of Logotherapy* (New York: The World Publishing Company, 1969), p. 50.

discover on his own through his personal experiences and choices of life. In order to find this meaning one has to confront his difficult and pressing moments of life with courage and responsibility. Personal awareness of life's meaning is essential because it offers the individual with a sense of direction and an understanding of the reason for his existence. Frankl has emphasized this idea by saying:

> ...There is nothing in the world, I venture to say, that would so effectively help one survive even the worst conditions, as the knowledge that there is a meaning in one's life. There is much wisdom in the words of Nietzssche: "He who has a *why* to live for can bear almost any *how*."[86]

From the above it is clear that the realization of one's meaning of life is the major driving force in one's existence. Frankl is particularly concerned with this understanding because he claims that the twentieth–century person is experiencing a serious "existential frustration" due to the lack of a meaning in life. He has further negated the assumption that material success can make one's living more meaningful. Material accomplishment alone does not provide real happiness in life, and Frankl has elaborated on this issue by explaining that:

---

[86] Viktor E. Frankl, *Man's Search for Meaning: An Introduction to Logotherapy* (New York: Washington Square Press, Inc., 1963), p. 164.

> ...the dream that if we just improve the socioeconomic situation of people, everything will be okay, people will become happy. The truth is that as the struggle for survival has subsided, the question has emerged: survival for what? Ever more people today have the means to live, but no meaning to live.[87]

Socioeconomic gains and the technological advances in some countries of the world has enhanced the quantity of life but it has produced an inverse effect on the quality of life. In fact we notice that people in these countries have become more aggressive and resort to belligerence or litigations very easily and have lost the traditional values of life. For instance, Japan has become a major economic power in the world today and has made exceptional strides in industry and technology, but what happened in the subways there recently (the poison gas) is indicative of some serious human deficiency. Such an incidence of violence does not live up to traditional Japanese values. By large the Japanese people are Buddhist, and according to that faith human life is highly sacred. Why did the pendulum of sacrosanctity shift to the act of violence? Could this be symptomatic of an existential vacuum? Apart from the post–World War II material success, there remains an inner vacuum among the present Japanese generation which has not been equally fulfilled and they are

---

[87] Viktor E. Frankl, *The Unheard Cry for Meaning: Psychotherapy and Humanism* (New York: Simon and Schuster, 1978), p. 21.

somewhat confused about their cause for existence. Hard work has satisfied their basic needs but there is something beyond the comforts of high–tech which is lacking. The discovery of this missing link comes through personal intentional inquisitiveness, and one should question the cause for existence beyond material accomplishments. To question one's meaning of life is not representative of a sickness but a deep–rooted human concern. In reference to this Frankl says:

> ...man's concern about a meaning in life which should be worthy of life, is in itself by no means a sign of disease ... this is an intrinsically human question. Challenging the meaning of life can, therefore, never be taken as a manifestation of morbidity or abnormality.[88]

Throughout his writings, Frankl has stressed that an individual must make his life more meaningful by constantly making an effort to discover the ultimate meaning of his existence. In fact he even goes further by saying that a human being alone has the capacity to question the meaning of his life for this meaning is not accessible to lower species as they do not have the potential to question the meaning for their existence.[89]

Frankl is of the opinion that life can be made meaningful in a threefold way:

---

[88] Viktor E. Frankl, "On Logotherapy and Existential Analysis," *American Journal of Psychoanalysis* XVIII (1958), 29.
[89] Ibid., 32.

> ... first, through what we give to life;
> second, by what we take from the
> world; and third, through the stand
> we take toward a fate we no longer
> can change.[90]

If one can acquire the meaning of life through the realization of these three approaches, then what are the appropriate directions? In response to this question, Frankl maintains that an individual puts meaning into his own life by being creative; by being receptive to the world and nature; and by taking a courageous stand toward extremely distressing circumstances of one's life.[91] Logotherapy, thus, is value–oriented, and it suggests that the ultimate meaning of one's life can be discovered by internalizing these three values. Such values are realized when man makes an effort to work for the benefit of others, experiences the joy of nature, and courageously faces his life's misfortunes.[92] In reality these are the values that make existence truly worthwhile. Meaning of life is discovered through personal challenges and demanding situations, and these circumstances most often provide opportunities to find one's worth. As Frankl has affirmed:

> ...Life is never lacking a meaning. ... we
> may also find meaning in life even

---

[90] Viktor E. Frankl, *Psychotherapy and Existentialism: Selected Papers on Logotherapy* (New York: Washington Square Press, Inc., 1967), p. 15.

[91] Arthur G. Wirth, "A search for Meaning," *Improving College and University Teaching*, IX (1961), p. 157.

[92] Edith Weisskopf-Joelson, "Logotherapy and Existential Analysis," *Acta Psychotherapeutica*, VI (1958), p. 194.

> when confronted with a hopeless sit-
> uation as its helpless victim, when
> facing a fate that cannot be changed.
> For what then counts and matters is
> to bear witness to the uniquely
> human potential at its best, which is
> to transform a tragedy into a person-
> al triumph, ...[93]

Thus this value–oriented approach in logotherapy goes beyond the psychodynamic and psycho-
genetic perspectives.[94] Explicitly, then, meaning of
life can only be understood through the realization
of tasks which are anchored to some significant values or a responsible cause. This cause intrinsically
has a transcending quality and is not meant to benefit oneself.[95] In this search for meaning, man,
according to Frankl, is guided by his conscience;
that is, his intuitive capacity[96]. Frankl has described
the concept of conscience and intuitive capacity in
these words:

> ...Conscience could be defined as
> the intuitive capacity of man to find
> out the meaning of a situation. Since
> this meaning is something unique, it
> does not fall under a general law,
> and an intuitive capacity such as

---

[93] Viktor E. Frankl, *The Unheard Cry for Meaning: Psychotherapy and Humanism* (New York: Simon and Schuster, 1978), p. 39.

[94] Viktor E. Frankl, "Psychiatry and Man's Quest for Meaning," *Journal of Religion and Health*, I (1961-62), p. 94.

[95] Viktor E. Frankl, "What is Meant by Meaning?" *Journal of Existentialism*, VII (1966- 67), p. 21.

[96] *Ibid.*, 26.

> conscience is the only means to seize
> hold of meaning. ....[97]

This may be interpreted to mean that conscience and life's meaning get interwoven into the individual's psychological fabric as significant values and the major guiding force in his or her creative thinking. Our intuitive thoughts and actions facilitate the realization of this unique meaning of existence. Conscience, then, is an internal capacity and an insight that assists in the comprehension of one's meaning of life. Frankl has carefully explained that conscience should not be equated to the concept of superego, because conscience in the context of logotherapy owns the capacity to oppose traditions and values that do not evince a significant meaningful end.[98] Life experiences, too, remind us that existential inadequacies which bear transcending values cannot be fulfilled by mandatory procedures. Besides unlike cultural traditions meaning of life not only varies from person to person but it also changes from situation to situation, as Frankl has expressed:

> ... meaning differs in two respects:
> first, from man to man, and second,
> from day to day — indeed, from hour
> to hour. ... There is, therefore, no such
> thing as a universal meaning of life,
> but only the unique meaning of indi-
> vidual situations.[99]

---

[97] Viktor E. Frankl, *The Will to Meaning: Foundations and Applications of Logotherapy* (New York: The World Publishing Company, 1969), p. 63.

[98] *Ibid.*, p. 19.

[99] Viktor E. Frankl, "What is Meant by Meaning?" *Journal of Existentialism*, VII (1966- 67), 22.

This means that in Frankl's judgment one cannot speak of the meaning of life in universal terms, and also, it is frivolous to conceive of meaning in a fixed pattern or tradition. As each person is unique, therefore, the meaning of life should also be consistent to this individual variations and not envisioned as a global thing. In fact at present we are living in a world in which societal traditions and values are very fluid and ephemeral, and at times it appears as if people have no direction to follow and show symptoms of lassitude. However, without question, there are aspects of one's existence which do have some common grounds with one another but the ultimate mission of life is very personal. As Frankl has remarked:

> Everyone has his own specific vocation of mission in life; everyone must carry out a concrete assignment that demands fulfillment. Therein he cannot be replaced, nor can his life be repeated.[100]

The foregoing remarks of Frankl also point to the fact that each human life is not only irreplaceable but also unrepeatable; therefore it signifies that every individual has a unique task to accomplish in her or his own given life span. Such an optimistic view of individual life has an inherent quality of self–worth and refers to a course of responsibility. It also means that every person in his own definitive way has a cause to fulfill and the mere longevity of life has no significance

---

[100] Viktor E. Frankl, *Man's Search for Meaning: An Introduction to Logotherapy* (New York: Washington Square Press, Inc., 1963), p. 172.

otherwise. According to the tenets of logotherapy, the fulfillment of some worthwhile task in life is more important than the total length of one's existence.[101]

Another outstanding feature of logotherapy is that even the suffering of life is assumed to have a significant place in human existence and entails an associated worthy purpose. To extend this perspective Edith Weisskopf–Joelson has very aptly remarked: "Since suffering is unavoidable, it seems much wiser to adopt a philosophy of life which accepts a certain amount of suffering or even gives it a positive value."[102] In both of the views suffering is professed to have a purpose of its own and it is not considered to be deleterious in effect. Thus by attributing a meaningful value to human suffering a person can alleviate the distressful aspect of it and deal with it more courageously. Frankl believes that a positive attitude toward one's suffering can actually transform the suffering into some exalting experience and has supported his point of view by quoting Goethe: "There is no condition which cannot be ennobled either by a deed or by suffering."[103] Such a conception of life certainly assists people who are experiencing an inner void and believe that their existence is devoid of any meaning but suffering.

From all the preceding discussions, one may come to realize that at one time or another, each of us is bound to question himself or herself about the

[101] Donald F. Tweedie, *Logotherapy and the Christian Faith* (Grand Rapids, Michigan: Baker Book House, 1961), p. 135.

[102] Edith Weisskopf-Joelson, "Some Comments on a Viennese School of Psychiatry," *Journal of Abnormal and Social Psychology,* LI (July-November, 1995), 702.

[103] Viktor E. Frankl, "On Logotherapy and Existential Analysis," *American Journal of Psychoanalysis* XVIII (1958), 32.

ultimate goal of his or her life and its real meaning. A response to this question varies with individual perspective and his mental makeup. The goal of life has been interpreted by some to achieve material wealth and personal status, or satisfying the organismic needs, or to serve the mankind and its creator the God. Whatever the goal one may conceive, in the final analysis, the underlying motive of each individual is to discover the specific direction and purpose for his existence, but this cannot be realized without a meaningful orientation. In essence one must make an effort to discover the goal of his life with serious determination and not with a fearful uncertainty that can mute one's creative capacities and obliterate one's worth.

IV. God and Logotherapy

In logotherapy Frankl has made a place for a person's faith in God and has given the spiritual core of a person considerable importance. Frankl observes an orderly relationship between a person and the spiritual world. He has never deliberately attempted to trespass the domain of the divine world with any bias and has left his theory open to all religious faiths and beliefs. Since Frankl is very insistent in claiming that man is continuously struggling to find a meaning of his life, then, what is this meaning after all? In reply to this question, Frankl says, "Man's search for meaning is enhanced by the innate, deep-rooted groping for the Ultimate, the Supra-meaning."[104] Frankl asserts that man can reach out for this Ultimate meaning by having trust in some higher supernatural existence or force, and this may be interpreted to be the God to him. This shows that God exists as a living reality for Frankl. A logotherapist, therefore, heightens a person's thinking to the level of transcendence wherein he has the chance to discover the ultimate meaning of his existence.[105] This kind of mental elevation increases the potentialities to comprehend the latent supra-human realities. In the context of logotherapy a person's behavior is not dictated by any specific faith or religious beliefs; instead, it is left up to the individual to discover his own faith that will eventually govern his thoughts and actions in life. Such a secular approach is very worldly and embraces the entire

---

[104] Viktor E. Frankl, "Religion and Existential Psychotherapy," *Gordon Review*, VI (1960), 6.

[105] Viktor E. Frankl, *The Will to Meaning: Foundations and Applications of Logotherapy* (New York: The World Publishing Company, 1969), p. 151.

global community. Frankl further insists that logotherapy is not a religious system per se or a technique of preaching.[106]

Whereas speaking about the existence of God, Frankl claims that one cannot prove the existence of a supernatural being because God is no petrification.[107] He has very aptly substantiated his viewpoint by saying that the existence of God cannot be determined by unfolding the historical stratification of the earth. According to Frankl, the existence of supernatural force can only be observed through individual but personal life experiences and not by elaborated laboratory experimental designs. Frankl further asserts that one does not have to prove that two and two make four; in fact, such realities are discovered through independent endeavors.[108] From Frankl's perspective, the realization of supernatural existence or God is accomplished by striving for some higher cause in life. Frankl claims that man struggles to reach out for individual spiritual answers not because of any moral motive and drive but for the sake of his own God.[109] This intent of reaching out has been perceived as analogous to transcendence in logotherapy.

Frankl further maintains that man cannot speak of God, but he may speak to God through his personal prayers; in other words, by reaching out to Him

---

[106] Donald F. Tweedie, *Logotherapy and the Christian Faith: An Evaluation of Frankl's Existential Approach to Psychotherapy* (Michigan: Baker Book House, 1961), p. 148.

[107] Viktor E. Frankl, *The Will to Meaning: Foundations and Applications of Logotherapy* (New York: The World Publishing Company, 1969), p. 148.

[108] Viktor E. Frankl, *The Doctor and the Soul: From Psychotherapy to Logotherapy* (New York: Alfred A. Knopf, Inc., 1965), p. xviii.

[109] Viktor E. Frankl, *Man's Search for Meaning: An Introduction to Logotherapy* (New York: Washington Square Press, 1963), p. 158.

through personal convictions or commitments.[110] In Frankl's thinking, man has the capacity to discover the latent supra–human realities through his actions and deeds. Meaningful deeds or tasks of some worth are the ones that uplift a person to these superior realities. The discovery of spiritual (noological) reality, at times, is accidental and stems from circumstances that are perhaps both mentally and physically distressful, such as being a prisoner of a war, having a mental break-down, or a major medical disability. In fact, these are the conditions that create an opportunity for a person to transcend himself and reach out to discover the ulti-mate meaning of life through challenging but respon-sible endeavors. Every person has an earnest need to discover this hidden reality. As Frankl claims:

> There is, in fact, a religious sense deeply rooted in each and every man's unconscious depths. ... that this sense may break through unex-pectedly even in cases of severe men-tal illness or prison ...[111]

This may also be interpreted to mean that man has the inherent capacity and quality to search for his hidden worth; and thus, fulfill a meaningful existence that will finally elevate him to a spiritual destination.

Frankl sees man reaching out for religious aware-ness through his personal zeal and decisions rather than driven by his unconscious instincts, and this

---

[110]Viktor E. Frankl, *The Will to Meaning: Foundations and Applications of Logotherapy* (New York: The World Publishing Company, 1969), p. 146.

[111] Viktor E. Frankl, *The Unconscious God* (New York: Simon and Schuster, 1975), p. 11.

perspective stands in direct conflict with Carl G. Jung. Frankl claims that Jung has overlooked the essential transcendental quality of the spiritual (noological) dimension in man by placing the religious endeavors of man among the category of instincts and drives.[112] Frankl asserts that man intentionally establishes a relationship between himself and a specific faith because he sees that it is the only way to realize the ultimate meaning of life. In contrast Jung saw the archetypal God image in the unconscious layers of man and not in personal meaningful commitments.

Frankl's logotherapy is based on scientific grounds, but it certainly does not destroy and undermine the religious aspirations of man. Frankl does not commit publicly who his God is, but he does not deny the existence of God either. Frankl definitely prefers some form of religious commitment to nihilism; however, he leaves it to the individual to decide in the selection of his or her personal faith. Frankl has suggested that, if religion is to survive, it will have to be profoundly personalized.[113] Such a philosophical position fits into present day thinking and offers reasonable leverage to most persons concerning their belief in God. At least it is not dictational and recognizes individual's freedom to choose as desired. Frankl's own religious background is Jewish, but he has never shown any religious bias in his writings. As a matter of fact, his wife and daughter are both Catholics. To Frankl belief in God and commitment to a religious faith is expected to be unconditional and he thinks that these personal convictions get further strengthened by life's predicaments and

[112] Tweedie, *op. cit.*, 48.

[113] Viktor E. Frankl, *The Unconscious God* (New York: Simon and Schuster, 1975), p. 15.

catastrophes.[114] In some ways, the challenges of life do facilitate this spiritual discovery and lend to the phenomenological condition of self–awareness. Frankl's logotherapy relies on the noological (noetic) approach, and he has given a special place to the spiritual need of a person. In order to fully understand Frankl's position on individual's belief or spirituality one must make an attempt to evaluate his conception of a person.

In the context of logotherapy, a person is viewed as an entity complete in itself; that is, a free and responsible being who is always striving for some meaningful goals. Throughout his writings Frankl has retained the wholeness of a person and has successfully avoided engaging into a serious dichotomy. In Frankl's dimensional model (somatic, psychic, and noetic), the spiritual part of a person is assumed to be beyond one's self and is not implied to have any theological connotation. Frankl further asserts that the spiritual element is precisely that constituent which is primarily responsible for the unity of a person.[115] Even though Frankl has proposed a three–dimensional view of a person he has made no specific attempt to reduce the wholeness of a person. Just as the Gestalt psychologists speak of the "whole" as more important than the sum of its separate elements, so has Frankl suggested that in the ultimate analysis a person must not be viewed as composed of separate parts but as an organismic whole. In essence, Frankl is very adamant in maintaining both the unity and the wholeness of a person. Besides, Frankl considers each

---

[114] *Ibid.*, p. 16.

[115] Viktor E. Frankl, "Religion and Existential Psychotherapy," *Gordon Review,* VI (1960), p. 2.

person to be unique and worthwhile and recognizes individual distinction and dignity. Frankl admits that human endeavors, very often, may not necessarily lead to a productive meaningful end; however, it is the trying in life rather than withdrawing from the challenges of life that truly make up for the personal worth and dignity. In view of the mundane challenges Frankl does not isolate the person from his or her given societal station; instead, he maintains that in one way or the other, a person is subject to social censorship, and therefore cannot discover his or her spiritual self by societal separation and exclusion. Frankl would prefer to see a community of responsible persons and not a mere mass of depersonalized isolated entities. The discovery of individual spirituality rests within the "social nexus" and is closely interwoven to it. Frankl further stresses that in order to be authentic in one's thoughts and actions, a person must also show courage to take a stand against those restricted religious propagations which promote prejudice and social bias, and one should not seek an escape from such self–serving group interests. Self–absorbing personal beliefs may lack responsibility and eventually could lead to self–enclosure, and also, distance a person from the realities of life.

In logotherapy, Frankl has attempted to present the image of a person as an integral part of the total society and yet has cautiously maintained that the personal growth of an individual should not be limited by the society. He believes that the individual development must not be restricted by the collective bond because it stifles personal creativity and uniqueness. History has proven that societies with closed systems, in the long range, can lend to the destruction of individual spirit and intellectual diversity. Frankl believes that in the final analysis, it is the person who as a *being* decides either to descend to the level of an animal or to ascend to the life of a saint.[116] Thus, it is the person who truly possesses the potential to select between good and bad, and it is the person who in the end determines the direction of his or her own spirituality. Logotherapy aims at uplifting each person to the highest possible level of achievement and worth. Frankl proposes to each individual to see life as a unique assignment which should be discovered and eventually fulfilled.[117] He recognizes the fact that human beings are bound to make mistakes in the process of this self–discovery but it should not present any major concern.

Logotherapy is an open–ended philosophy which has gained a world–wide following because it does not require any specific moral alliance or identification. It emphasizes that it is the person who determines the direction of his or her own life, subject to his personal frame of references; which could be the society, conscience, or God.[118] Thus, Frankl recognizes the mutual relationship between the individual and the society — an inseparable reality. When a society is in a state of metamorphosis, it may appear as if humans have lost vision of their spiritual responsibility and are distanced from their ultimate mission of life, but

---

[116] Viktor E. Frankl, *Psychotherapy and Existentialism: Selected Papers on Logotherapy* (New York: Washington Square Press, Inc., 1967), p. 110.

[117] Viktor E. Frankl, *The Doctor and the Soul: From Psychotherapy to Logotherapy* (New York: Alfred A. Knopf, Inc., 1965), p. 55.

[118] Viktor E. Frankl , *The Will to Meaning: Foundations and Applications of Logotherapy* (New York: The World Publishing Company, 1969), p. 143.

this is not the case. In fact, the turbulent periods most often evolve into peaceful cosmic lights leading to a more productive meaningful end, and one should realize that society as a larger entity has the resilience to absorb periodic deviations and finally revert to an orderly whole.

In short, logotherapy places an equal emphasis on the discovery of one's personal affinity to God and the divine world and encourages the person to contemplate on ideas pertaining to the supreme force. Frankl's perspective of human growth is based on the principle of a unified whole and his approach is integrative of body, mind, and spirit. Logotherapy is very inclusive, and its ideas and concepts can easily be extended to other specific areas and activities of life. Today's educators the world over are concerned about providing meaningful education to students; therefore the following discussion will clearly portray how the principles of logotherapy can be incorporated in the process of learning and education.

V. Logotherapy and Education

In this age of high technological exuberance and global economic competition, educators cannot be content with transmitting traditional heritage and textbook education to their students. They have to provide intellectual challenges, experiences, and skills which will enable them to sieve out somber temptations that may precipitate from the material affluence. Young folks need to comprehend that exaggerated material successes have the potential to mitigate human values and increase social problems to some extent. Changes in family lifestyles and the structural unit have caused additional demands on the young minds, and they have to make decisions that are quite stressful at times. Thus contemporary youth is more vulnerable to the pressures of living. Education by large has not been able to cope with these increasing social challenges and in some instances has failed to provide crucial skills vital to making independent and responsible decisions. Factual knowledge has failed to serve the youth in a meaningful way, and as a result, frustrations related to these intellectual deficiencies are clearly visible in their lives. For example, the youth violence and aggression. Wholesome living requires a balanced understanding of the past and the present, and an active exposure to life experiences that are very try-ing. Hence, educators today have a serious concern to prepare the young mind who is well equipped to filter out exaggerated claims of television commer-cials and similar situations which promote faulty understandings. Schools need to cultivate among students the process of decision making and encourage them to participate in experiences that could enhance their capacity to make meaningful selections among available alternatives. Intellectual textbook activities alone do not assist the learner to visualize the hazards of living, one requires firsthand encounters to internalize the harsh realities of life. Educators need to widen the inner vision and strengths and stimulate the students to develop their individual conscience. Frankl believes that education must develop the conscience of a person because it is this human conscience that generally guides in the selection of a choice.[119]

Technological accomplishments have created "informational highways," and as a result, today's youth is more knowledgeable and well–informed. The youth of today does not easily accept any repository of traditional wisdom *verbatim–et–literatim* and does not hesitate to pose an intellectual confrontation to ideas that profess rigid thinking. They have an astute mind and are more open to logical academic controversies. Today's youth cannot be treated as a person whose behavior can be easily manipulated by predetermined ideas and plans. In view of this, logotherapy is opposed to a deterministic philosophy and suggests that if educators fail to recognize individual freedom, then the process of learning or education becomes an illusion.[120] Thus, any attempt to depersonalize students and view them as objects of manipulation will lead to academic failures. Students

---

[119] Viktor E. Frankl, *The Will to Meaning: Foundations and Application of Logotherapy* (New York: The World Publishing Company, 1969), p. 65.

[120] Viktor E. Frankl, *Man's Search For Meaning: An Introduction to Logotherapy* (New York: Washington Square Press, Inc., 1963), p. 209.

actively exercise their free *will* and are constantly changing in their outlook towards life, even their capacity to imbibe information, at times take sharp turns. Thus, their behavior is highly unpredictable and uncontrollable. In this regard Frankl says:

> ... every human being has the freedom to change at any instant. Therefore, we can only predict his future within the large frame of a statistical survey referring to a whole group; the individual personality however, remains essentially unpredictable.[121]

The above statement is indicative of the flexibility of human mind and explains why a person may respond to a similar situation differently at different times. In contrast to the behavioristic approach, in which the student is viewed as controllable, Frankl sees the student as free and responsible for his own learnings. Carl R. Rogers, too, has confirmed Frankl's thinking in his book, *Freedom to Learn*.[122] This reminds us that while planning for an education program the proponents of educational intents must take into account the concept of human free will and make provisions for individual freedom and diversity. Besides, they should acknowledge that students have a mind of their own to evaluate academic presentation; and thus, they cannot be muted by a predetermined approach as planned in advance.

---

[121] Viktor E. Frankl, "Basic Concepts of Logotherapy," *Journal of Existential Psychiatry,* III (1962), p. 116.

[122] Carl R. Rogers, *Freedom to Learn* (Columbus, Ohio: Charles E. Merrill Publishing Company, 1969), p. 268.

Educators may specify materials and methods, and make recommendations to bring forth changes in learner's behavior, but the end results can only be achieved if the learner is willingly receptive to such proposals. Educators can systematically guide the learners toward a goal but they cannot impose their intentions by force on the *will* of the learners. In view of this contention educators can help the students to realize that they are not powerless in the process of learning and they do have an equal control over their conditions of learning because they have the freedom to either accept or reject situational persuasions. Educators could provide challenges to their students to comprehend that they do possess the capacity to exercise their *free will* which can either facilitate or inhibit learning. In sum a person's future development depends on the manner in which he or she executes this free will, that is, in a responsible or destructive way. Students need to understand that the emancipation of their unique worth is closely tied to a constructive use of this free will. It is this individual capacity that enables the person to surmount hereditary and environmental limitations. Thus, a person is self-determining and has the ability to shape his or her future by discretely exercising the *free will*.

No doubt each student's behavior is influenced by the environment of a school but a student too is actively shaping the school's environment through his unique characteristics and participation; and thus the learner gets an added opportunity to experience how to use one's freedom constructively and change what is inappropriate. Self-assertion does not carry much weight if it is not expressed in a meaningful way. Participatory academic experience offer the learner to internalize the thin cleavage between free will and responsibility. Permissive environment is meaningful only if it leads to the creation of responsible outcomes. In brief the aim of education should then be to develop in each individual a level of consciousness that will enable him or her to exercise their personal freedom in a way that will enhance individual worth and yet preserve the dignity of others around. Frankl has very aptly synthesized his views on human freedom by saying that the Statue of Liberty on the East Coast of the United States should be supplemented by a Statue of Responsibility on the West Coast.[123]

A meaningful education is expected to develop in an individual the ability to appraise the consequences of his actions and decisions. When a person thinks of seeking freedom from his given circumstances, he should not fail to contemplate that every free action carries with it a corresponding sense of responsibility; otherwise life can become chaotic and a possibility of self–annihilation. The technological advances of today have a serious risk for misuse; therefore, it is expected that we place a heavy premium on responsibility. Generally speaking one may believe that the culture of a society in which a person lives controls the direction of his or her future growth, but one could easily miss the reality that the individual himself is the principal player in shaping his future.

In short, Frankl has taken a firm stand against rigid determinism and is opposed to the view that

---

[123] Viktor E. Frankl, *The Will to Meaning: Foundations and Applications of Logotherapy* (New York: The World Publishing Company, 1969), p. 49.

disregards a person's potential to influence his conditions. He claims that regardless of the conditions which circumstances present him, the individual under most conditions, has the freedom to decide for himself. A person is free to choose, but in each choice he is assuming complete responsibility for his actions. The most significant message to the educators that emerges from this concept of Frankl is the picture of a learner — free and responsible for his actions and decisions. Educators will not cover much distance in the process of learning if they tend to view the learner as passive recipient of predesigned plans climaxing to some predictable outcomes.

VI. Application of Logotherapy to Life

Frankl claims that humans are purposive in their efforts and intentions, and their behavioral pursuits cannot be interpreted in terms of predetermined predictable operations. Humans are creative thinkers and vary in their actions and responses. Each individual considers his life to be worthy of some specific meaning or purpose, and a failure to discover this purpose could make life boring and frustrating. To some extent, today, this lack of meaningful purpose in life has contributed to the high incidence of drug abuse and other social evils. A mental deficiency of this inner worth can lead to a sense of emptiness in life, especially when the social milieu fails to provide challenges that will help to emancipate this unique worth, otherwise hopelessness, and drudgery prevails (possibly eventuating into social deviations). To salvage this human despair, society should take initiatives to create opportunities that will encourage and enhance the discovery of this inner purpose or else risk individual alienation and withdrawal. We need to activate the hidden potentials of a person and avoid accepting his personal assumption about his limited capacity or an under–estimation of his self–worth and qualities. Goethe, a great writer of the past, once remarked: "If we take people as they are, we make them worse. If we treat them as if they were what they ought to be, we help them to become what they are capable of becoming."[124] At times, it is helpful to push back the goalposts and raise the performance expectations.

---

[124] Lawrence A. Pervin, "Existentialism, Psychology, and Psychotherapy," *American Psychologist,* XV (1960), 308.

Humans have the resilience to exceed their normal energies under conditions that are challenging and have demonstrated extraordinary feats. A person's lack of confidence in himself or low self–esteem could prompt him to profess satisfaction in achieving frivolous goals; however, this is not how one should embark on the journeys of life. Relegating oneself to a level of insignificance may produce mental anguish and a state of lassitude.

Frankl, too, was compelled to confront the question of life's meaning because of his personal experiences as an inmate of Nazi concentration camps and because of the problems he encountered in the daily lives of his patients as a psychiatrist. These factors influenced him to assume the *meaning of life* as one of the major tenets of logotherapy.

> Day by day I am confronted with people ... I am besieged by their cry for an answer to the question of an ultimate meaning to suffering.

> I myself went through this purgatory when I found myself in a concentration camp ... I asked myself what my life had been for ... but after wrestling with my despair for hours, ... if there is meaning, it is unconditional meaning, and neither suffering nor dying can detract from it.[125]

---

[125] Viktor E. Frankl, *The Will to Meaning: Foundations and Applications of Logotherapy* (New York: The World Publishing Company, 1969), pp. 155-56.

In actuality, Frankl's own life acquired meaning when the manuscript of his first book, *The Doctor and the Soul: An Introduction to Logotherapy*,[126] was confiscated by the Nazis during his stay in the concentration camps. The goal to accomplish this task of writing anew helped him to survive the atrocities of the Nazi camps. Under the influence of these unfortunate circumstances, Frankl discovered the purpose of his life. These WWII experiences led him to assume that the most basic human problem in the contemporary society is the individual's concern for finding the real meaning of his own existence. Frankl has emphasized that the *meaning* of each individual existence is most often determined by the demands of a given circumstance, and it is futile to predetermine one's life goals.[127] In this age, it is simply not possible to plan one's life tasks in advance without giving due consideration to constantly changing nature of the modern world. Hence, each given moment of life has a specific meaning of its own.[128] Life conditions are very complex today and they take sharp turns around. Frankl has attempted to resolve the problem of this meaning of life by suggesting that it is improper to seek an answer to this concern by directly questioning a person: "What is the meaning of your life?" Instead, Frankl has proposed an alternative to this question in these words:

> ... man should not ask what he may
> expect from life, but should rather

---

[126] Viktor E. Frankl, *Man's Search for Meaning: An Introduction to Logotherapy* (New York: Washington Square Press, Inc., 1963), p. 165.

[127] *Ibid.*, p. 172.

[128] *Ibid.*, p. 171.

> understand that life expects some-
> thing from him. It may also be put
> this way: in the last resort, man
> should not ask "What is the meaning
> of my life?" but should realize that
> he himself is being questioned. Life is
> putting its problems to him, and it is
> up to him to respond to these ques-
> tions by being responsible; he can
> only answer to life by answering for
> his life.[129]

This implies that one must not expect something from life rather one should question oneself: What must I do in order to make my life more meaningful and worthwhile? From Frankl's point of view, life is an opportunity to accomplish some meaningful goal, and there is a special meaning in every existence; however, its discovery rests upon the individual. Life is a challenge, and it does offer opportunities to prove one's worth; the two are so closely juxtaposed.

In Frankl's judgment, since a person is the prime recipient of life, it is he who is expected to give meaning to his own existence and destiny. Meaning cannot be assigned to a person arbitrarily; however, such a task is feasible and within the capacity of human reach. For instance, a person who lives a responsible life is capable of achieving this inner meaning of life. Contrarily a person who is overly concerned in the gratification of pleasurable motives gets distanced from life's meaning. In fact those who conceive the

---

[129] Viktor E. Frankl, *The Doctor and the Soul: From Psychotherapy to Logotherapy* (New York: Alfred A. Knopf, Inc., 1965), p. XV.

acquisition of material or pleasurable goals as the primary purpose of their existence are most likely not conscious of their inner worth. Such people appear to be confused, distressed, and even grisly in their own actions. Frankl, too, has alluded to this myopic approach by saying, "When we set up pleasure as the meaning of life, we insure that in the final analysis life shall inevitably seem meaningless."[130] Besides one should be mindful of the fact that the glamours of a mass of wealth, and/or the satisfaction of tissue needs, seldom bear a long–lasting meaning. Human history has ample examples to validate this opinion. We humans have a much higher purpose in our existence and we earnestly desire to make our living worthwhile. Such an expectation is woven into cultural fabrics of most societies. To mediate the contentious battle between acquiring material gains and fulfilling transcending needs is a real challenge for we humans. A person may choose to escape from this demand or confront it with fortitude. Life, certainly, has a specific purpose, and it is the awareness of this specific purpose, that becomes the real challenge in life because this insight in the end will provide a person with the essential sense of direction and enlightenment to pursue his daily activities, finally culminating into a meaningful living. In view of this Frankl has emphasized that:

> There is nothing in the world, I venture to say, that would so effectively help one survive even the worst conditions, as the knowledge that there

[130]Viktor E. Frankl, *The Doctor and the Soul: From Psychotherapy to Logotherapy* (New York: Alfred A. Knopf, Inc., 1965), p. 37.

> is a meaning in one's life. There is much wisdom in the words of Nietzsche: "He who has a why to live for can bear almost any how."[131]

The significant postulate in the above statement is that one must have an understanding of the meaning of his life in order to live more responsibly and productively.

Frankl holds that it is not a sign of sickness to question the meaning of one's existence. In fact, he believes that humans alone have the capacity to question the meaning of their existence,[132] for this meaning is not accessible to lower animals since they do not possess the ability to question the purpose of their existence. Frankl further adds:

> Challenging the meaning of life can, therefore, never be taken as a manifestation of morbidity or abnormality. It is rather the truest expression of the state of being human, the mark of the most human nature in man.[133]

Throughout his writings, Frankl has stressed that every individual has a purpose in his existence, and one should be seriously committed to discover this rather than escaping from life's demand.

---

[131] Viktor E. Frankl, *Man's Search for Meaning: An Introduction to Logotherapy* (New York: Washington Square Press, Inc., 1963), p. 164.

[132] Viktor E. Frankl, "On Logotherapy and Existential Analysis," *American Journal of Psychoanalysis* XVIII (1958), 32.

[133] *Ibid.*, 29.

According to Frankl, life can be made meaningful in threefold ways, that is, first, through what we give to life; second, by what we take from the world; and third, through the stand we take toward a fate we no longer can change.[134] This lends to suggest that a person can acquire meaning through three different approaches or values. What are these values then? In response to this question, Frankl maintains that an individual puts meaning into his own life by being creative; by being receptive to the world and nature; and by taking a courageous stand toward extremely distressing circumstances of one's life.[135] Thus logotherapy is value–oriented and emphasizes that the meaning of one's existence is possible to realize through an approach that carries some higher values.

What worth is this life if the human energy is most often driven towards acquiring self–serving needs? We need to go beyond this tunnel–vision. For some the technological potentials of Cyberspace or the Internet are limited to acquiring no more than lower order needs resulting into feculent solutions. Such a gratification is pernicious, slovenly, and lacking in noetic values. Higher order values are accomplished only when a person makes an effort to work for the benefit of others, experiences the joy of nature, and courageously faces life's misfortunes.[136] Life is an opportunity to seek a worthy destination and one has to rise above lower levels of personal satisfaction.

[134] Viktor E. Frankl, *Psychotherapy and Existentialism: Selected Papers on Logotherapy* (New York: Washington Square Press, Inc., 1967), p. 15.

[135] Arthur G. Wirth, "A Search for Meaning," *Improving College and University Teaching*, IX (1961), p. 157.

[136] Edith Weisskopf-Joelson, "Logotherapy and Existential Analysis," *Acta Psychotherapeutica*, VI (1958), p. 194.

Human activities should be directed to the emancipation of a worthy cause otherwise life becomes a morbid routine. The question of what this cause should be is left open to an individual and there is no predetermined panacea nor it is accessible through collective bargaining. The selection of this cause should be representative of a higher purpose and beyond one's self gratification. In this connection, Frankl writes:

> Man ... does so for the sake of a cause
> to which he commits himself, or for a
> person whom he loves, or for the sake
> of his God ... simply to serve God.[137]

This statement offers reasonable magnitude to a person to seek a cause, and then, expects him to pursue it with firm commitment. Frankl believes that, being human always means to be directed to something other than oneself.[138]

While speaking of meaning, Frankl has assumed that each individual existence is unique, and therefore, the meaning of life varies from person to person. Furthermore, he believes that man is constantly in the process of a change, which implies that the meaning of life is subject to circumstantial variations as well. There are aspects of one's existence that are constant and common to each other, however, all humans intend to strive for a worthwhile fulfillment in life and in the end desire to leave behind prints of their significant contributions in a world of which they were

---

[137] Viktor E. Frankl, *Man's Search for Meaning: An Introduction to Logotherapy* (New York: Washington Square Press, Inc., 1963), p. 158.

[138] Viktor E. Frankl, "What is Meant by Meaning?" *Journal of Existentialism*, VII (1966- 67), 21.

once a part. Yet as the situations change, the meaning of one's existence could change along with the conditions. Just like a tropical tree in India may provide a person with the shade to protect from the hot sunshine, fruit for consumption, and fallen twigs as a source of fuel or energy for cooking. In each case here is the worth but the meaning corresponds to the situational demands.

One of the outstanding features of Frankl's conception of life is that he has given a vital place to human suffering by associating it to some higher cause and purpose in life. Edith Weisskopf-Joelson has very aptly recognized this point of view by remarking: "Since suffering is unavoidable, it seems much wiser to adopt a philosophy of life which accepts a certain amount of suffering or even gives it a positive value."[139] Thus by attributing human suffering to some meaningful cause, Frankl has employed an approach commonly used in most religions. He further believes that a positive attitude toward one's suffering can actually transform a person's misfortune into an ennobling experience. This attitude was adopted by a mother whose child was killed by a drunken driver, and consequentially she became an activist and a strong supporter of the MADD (Mothers Against Drunken Drivers) movement. Her creative and purposeful attitude led her to surmount her tragedy into a meaningful contribution to mankind. Frankl has further supported his position by quoting Goethe: "There is no condition which cannot be ennobled either by a deed or by

---

[139] Edith Weisskopf-Joelson, "Some Comments on a Viennese School of Psychiatry," *Journal of Abnormal and Social Psychology,* LI (July-November, 1955), 702.

suffering."[140] Such a conception of life will certainly assist people who are experiencing an inner void and believe that their existence is meaningless. In fact, in today's society a person finds it very difficult to transform his or her suffering into some meaningful purpose and may even fail to relate his or her suffering to a higher cause. However, there are a few exceptions, such as the actor Christopher Reeves, and they are the ones who never lose sight of the purpose for their existence. Adversities do not deter them, and their determination to make life meaningful gets further fortified by distressful events. They understand that life has a meaning even under circumstances that are very trying; they are committed to a cause and exercise a strong degree of control over the events of their fate with fortitude. I have had firsthand experiences of "trying times" and have lived through the atrocities of World War II in Singapore, and I do vividly remember the painful encounters met during the Japanese occupation of Singapore. Those experiences are inenarrable and consciously difficult to enumerate. I have tried my best to be oblivious of those and not to sustain any hostility against the Japanese. Life is worth more than brooding over the past grief, as a matter of fact, the miseries of World War II have made me more self-reliant, forgiving, and compassionate. Encounters of the War enabled me to discover my creative and responsible ability. I do not ruminate over the bitter memories because they produce mental anguish and mitigate my intellectual well-being. Besides I believe that the hardships of the past should

---

[140] Viktor E. Frankl, "On Logotherapy and Existential Analysis," *American Journal of Psychoanalysis*, XVIII (1958), 32.

be viewed as a springboard to jump forward and not to stifle the future growth by hatching over them. At times a person may use mental manipulations (faulty perceptions) to balm the sufferings of the past, which in the short-term could appear to be excusable as an escape but in the long-term such perceptions do not accomplish much and lend serious risk to mental health. Ill feelings reassert animosity, anger, hatred, and provide a motivational precursor to activate the violent energies.

Suffering is an integral part of life, and it constitutes an essential element of being human. Challenges of life create an opportunity to prove our selfworth and enduring resistance to difficult times makes a person hardier. Endurance may even mobilize hidden creative potentials that could be left dormant. A meaningful understanding of one's suffering requires realignment of our cognitive strategies. A person's inevitable suffering caused by some misfortune can be transformed into an achievement or a creative value by changing one's personal mental attitude toward his or her circumstance. Frankl has stressed that suffering ceases to be suffering when it finds a meaning.[141] Since each individual existence is unique and distinct, each life then is a new assignment and a task and requires new solutions and perceptions. Seeking a cultural sanctum from life's problems is not an appropriate choice. A person should be prepared to undergo hardships and sufferings in order to accomplish his or her life's special assignment, and there is a purpose in confronting one's unfortunate

---

[141] Viktor E. Frankl, "The Will to Meaning," *The Living Church,* CXLIV (June 24, 1962), p. 9.

conditions. A person should be productively engaged in his life irrespective of the conditions. As Nels F.S. Ferre has remarked. "The meaning of life finally is to participate as creatively, as fully, and as lastingly as possible in the concrete process in which one finds himself."[142]

Logotherapy is considered a psychotherapeutic technique to deal with human problems, and thus it assists in the healing of many emotional and mental disorders of a person.[143] It helps a person to change his personal mental attitude toward his unalterable condition. Logotherapy assists in encountering existential predicaments and through its use one may enlarge his or her vision to face the problems of life. Logotherapy has the motivational power to direct a person in his most crucial moments and lead him out of his existential dilemmas by providing him with a renewed zeal and a positive attitude toward his unchangeable circumstance. Logotherapy is positively an optimistic perspective because it provides a person with directions that can help him or her to rise above his or her moments of distress, Frankl insists that logotherapy is very realistic in life as it faces the tragic triad of human existence: pain, death, and guilt; and also it shows the person how to transform his despair into triumph.[144] Frankl's theory is truly realistic in approach; after all death and sufferings are part of human existence and it is appropriate to have a

---

[142] Nels F.S. Ferre, *A Theology for Christian Education* (Philadelphia, Pennsylvania: The Westminster Press, 1967), 85.

[143] Godfryd Kaczanowski, "Logotherapy - A New Psychotherapeutic Tool," *Psychosomatics*, VIII (May-June, 1967), p. 159.

[144] Viktor E. Frankl, *The Will to Meaning: Foundations and Applications of Logotherapy* (New York: The World Publishing Company, 1969), p. ix.

meaningful understanding of these aspects of life. In logotherapy, Frankl maintains that a person has the capacity to mold his situations into meaningful experiences even if he is deeply drowned in the ocean of despair and emptiness. Of course, a person is limited in changing his past but he can certainly influence in modifying his present and the future. Logotherapy refers to the need and understanding of meaningfulness in human thoughts and actions under all conditions of life. Physical limitations in no way restricted Helen Keller to rise above her conditions. Each person has his or her own share of discomfort and distress, and that is what life is all about. Self-pity leads to low self-esteem and frustration and could ensue negative mental attitude.

Each person spins to his own unique path of life, and each individual is expected to live through distinct life experiences. However, it is the quality of choice one opts for while living through these experiences that truly makes him different and meaningful. Every human life is representative of a meaning and has an inner capacity to surmount personal distress and handicaps by realizing the end purpose. Keniston has aptly written: "Men will happily tolerate great discomfort, discontinuity, and frustration if they are working for some purpose, toward some end, which they consider wise, true, exciting, and meaningful."[145] Good things are hard to come by easily but responsible goal–oriented commitment will emerge into a meaningful end. In essence Frankl has given a positive attribute to human suffering and considers it an integral part of meaningful living.

---

[145] Kenneth Keniston, "Alienation and the Decline of Utopia," *The American Scholar,* XXIX (1959-60), 181.

VII. Work and Meaning

Today's assembly-line workers are plagued with a sense of futility in performing the same job routines over and over. These daily work routines generate an inner feeling of detachment and helplessness, possibly resulting into work-related depression. Such feelings lead to low level of personal involvement, an attitude of resignation, and decreased motivational drive. Lack of intrinsic participation in these work routines is unhealthy because it does not provide the mental joy or satisfaction of work. The worker gets alienated from job assignment and begins to mentally experience worthlessness. On the other hand, when a worker makes an honest assessment of such a resigned behavior and lack of involvement in his or her job, it creates an inner conflict and subsequently a sense of guilt. When a person is not fully engaged in an effort it is bound to cause mental tension and frustration. In fact the contemporary worker is at a much higher risk for this type of mental distress because he experiences a perpetual fear of incompetence to fast-changing work related technologies. These technical changes induce a lack of personal control over work (for being inadequate in skills and knowledge). Besides there is an on-going concern for being laid off primarily because of the restructuring, down-sizing, or cost-effective trend among most organizations today. These concerns are mentally very stressful and damaging to health in the long range.

The problem here is that some workers experience the intensity of these anxiety-laden feelings more than others and as a result subject themselves to work–related illnesses. This phenomena of mental stress among workers is one of the major reasons for half–hearted involvement in work. Like most conflicts of life, job dissatisfaction creates a cognitive vacuum leading to meaninglessness and boredom. The intrinsic reward for work is missing, and thus it kills the internal energy. Such job–related deficiencies could cause a psychic disorder of neurasthenia and other psychosomatic symptoms among workers. In the context of Frankl's theory of Logotherapy such an illness is attributable to tensions that emerge from traditional values of work and the modern living.[146] The characteristics of such an illness are not directly related to one's primary needs; instead these are the consequences of a failure to discover a genuine meaning in what one is doing. This deficiency of purpose is bound to evolve when we treat workers as nothing more than mechanical objects and take solace in their being provided for the basic essentials. Workers, today, are seeking something beyond simple work routines, they are more educated and enlightened, they earnestly desire to use their personal creative potentials and energies to the fullest, and when this opportunity is missing, work loses the intrinsic value effecting into an inner emptiness and worthlessness. It triggers inner agitation and frustration and related mental anxieties. A worker begins to feel restricted because it does not offer the mental freedom to participate fully and experience actualization of one's potentials.

---

[146] Viktor E. Frankl, *Psychotherapy and Existentialism: Selected Papers on Logotherapy* (New York: A Clarion Book Company, 1967), p. 71.

This job frustration is a precursor to low motivational pattern among workers and it is the direct outcome of rapid automation and increased job insecurity. No doubt, automation has relieved the workers of redundant routines and laborious work procedures but simultaneously it has also created a sense of insignificance and mitigation of their personal control over work. At the same time, automation has also given them the benefit of added leisure hours but without the corresponding increase in personal resources to enjoy these additional leisure hours. Resources have not kept a parallel pace of increase, and this gap is mentally bothersome. It has become very expensive to enjoy the leisure time and the lack of potential to afford effects into individual jealousies and unhappiness of its own kind. To some extent, in dense urban living areas, these limitations of resources to enjoy the leisure time is responsible for excessive aggression and violence. Confinement of space and lack of recreational facilities or activities lead to mental inhibition and can generate negative energies. Neurologically the human mind is very active and has to be engaged productively or else one may run the risk of deviation in behavior. As it has been aptly remarked, an idle brain is the devil's workshop.

Feelings of meaninglessness, alienation, and apathy, with reduced sense of purpose and control over one's work assignment, and limitations over one's intent to be creative is quite common in technologically advanced urbanized societies of the world. In the highly industrialized countries the momentum of life has accelerated, day–to–day human activities have become more mechanical (both domestic and professional), and as a result the individual is experiencing a generalized sense of human insignificance. The absence of traditional values and the depersonalization of human effort has contributed to the pervasive condition of stress at work. Humans feel disengaged in their effort, both at home and outside. Job stress has become a problem due to the lack of this inner fulfillment and a sense of separation from work. This inner confusion and chaos within oneself is not a pathogenic illness, however it is an anxiety caused by one's conscience and the fear of failure to shoulder his or her social responsibilities of existence.[147] This anxiety progressively leads to the development of unproductive behaviors. Thus the failure of mental involvement in performing a task, as well as meaningful understanding of the purpose in its accomplishment, is a major dynamic force in job related illnesses. The awareness of purpose in what one is doing is crucial in order to maintain an inner harmony between human effort and the satisfaction of its outcome. This understanding can help to alleviate some of the anxieties of work and offer an opportunity to perform tasks that are eventually meaningful. However, a sense of purpose in doing something cannot be prescribed, and the ultimate decision to make one's job assignment truly meaningful rests with the worker. Company policies that are forced on people, for the sake of a common good, may end up in rejection and/or covert opposition. Besides

---

[147] E. Weisskoff-Joelson, "Logotherapy and Existential Analysis," *Acta Psychotherapeutica*, Vol. 6 No. 3 (1958), p. 197.

management does not alone own a monopoly of wisdom, it is only through an open mutual dialogue (the Greek word: dia meaning through, and logos stands for meaning), the real sense of purpose could be understood. The management can create an environment similar to a high tide which can promote conditions that will help many boats to float through shallow waters. However an understanding of one's own constructive role within an organization can best be realized by engaging in the decision–making process, by being creative, and by adopting a positive attitude towards one's job assignment.

Psychotherapeutic and other corrective measures in work–related stress cases may make an attempt to focus on personal attitudes, manufacturing and mechanical designs, work environment, and managerial sensitivities, but all these have limitations of their own. Prescription drugs cannot prevent or eliminate negative feelings nor is an escape a solution, but a realistic resolve to this problem is to encourage the workers to realize their unique individual contribution and significance in the completion of a specific task. Any attempt to chemically treat individuals suffering from job frustration and stress is in the long range futile and incomplete. Material rewards may provide a short term cure but they lack in the intrinsic value and the purpose of work.

A person experiencing a job frustration is usually bored and apathetic, therefore, he could be challenged to perform tasks that require high level of commitment, active engagement, and a degree of self–fulfillment. Tasks that promote a sense of purpose will certainly minimize job frustration and increase inner satisfaction and work pride, and thus enhance self–esteem.

VIII. Existence and Meaning

The contemporary material success has developed an attitude toward life in which extension of personal interest has become the primary driving force for some. Global love, care, peace, and an understanding of each other, the very paradigm of human coexistence, are being compromised in some ways. The mutual respect that bridges the human diversity and harmonious living appears to be resting on a soft ground these days. The crumbling traditional family values is making existence even more controversial, complex, and challenging in day-to-day living. Culturally impoverished families are finding it difficult to cope with the responsibilities of living, especially in a traditional context. Existence in itself is precarious enough, and the lack of a sound family value foundation is compounding life demands with increasing intricacies. The daily news agenda presents examples of human judgmental errors which are directly related to weak or ambivalence of human values. Some young minds are in complete disarray and have no understanding of traditional cultural values and responsibilities. A very close friend of mine recently confided in me and shared his most painful experience of life. My friend explained to me that because of some very uncompromising home conditions and personal conflicts pertaining to his beliefs, it became very difficult for him to adapt to an unexpected family demand. Thus he was feeling mentally very miserable. Under these circumstances he decided to speak to his adult educated son about his mental anguish, presuming that his son would extend his shoulder to lean on for support, but in return this is what his son said to his father, "Dad, if you are that miserable, then you find a solution for yourself, and I don't give a damn." When I heard this from my friend, at first I did not trust my ears and felt mentally devastated. I was dumbfounded and dazed for a few minutes and had no courage to make eye contact with my friend. This is the same son for whom the father had toiled so hard to put him through professional education of a highest degree and provided him with the maximum comfort of modern living as a student. As far as I know this son was given reasonable opportunity to gain an awareness and an insight of family responsibilities and expectations, and yet he showed no regard for those values because for all the years he was away during the course of his professional education he failed to develop a real meaningful set of values on his own. Many young people today do not understand the emotional significance and an in depth meaning of family values and love. The growing youth lacks internalizing that family's material achievements and economic affluence alone cannot guarantee a mental state of well-being, stability, or happiness. While growing up we need to realize that the sense of personal fulfillment and inner peace can only be accomplished through a meaningful and purposeful living. Material objects are nothing more than the basic sources of self-survival and we need something more than these perishable products to connect ourselves to the higher levels of humanity. A person in his or her own self-search, should at least have a clear delineation of what could enhance or inhibit a meaningful existence. Externally we can make provisions for the young mind to observe between the right and the wrong but there is no way to impose the acceptance of these values in a free society. Since values are relative to the context of living, they too are subject to change and reexamination. Besides in today's world we are intensely pressured to recognize an individual's right to possess his or her own beliefs or values. Therefore, it is only rational to expect that humans should have some conception of values which in the long range are representative of a transcendental dimension. In creating individual beliefs and values a person should at least consider asking herself or himself how would these eventuate in making her or his life more sublime and worthy. On the contrary, an ill–conceived set of values can lead to despair and self–destruction. I have no intention of suggesting any specific model of ethical codes because personal values are highly subjective and are not characterized by any degree of limitations. Moreover, human actions and responses are at times unpredictable, and it is difficult to provide some definitive value orientation that may eventually evolve into self–transcendence. Societies in the past have functioned according to established cultural traditions and ethical codes but today there is an increasing reevaluation of traditions and mores. At present we are in a constant state of flux and standards of behavior appear to be very fluid. Changes are quite common and apparently in concurrence with the realities of contemporary living. Individual rights are increasingly overshadowing cultural traditions, for instance, the physician–assisted suicides of Dr. Jack Kevorkian do not match with the past societal traditions. Such changes have become complex judicial and societal controversies. These are inescapable realities of existence today, but one curiously wonders if our lives can be propagated *ad infinitum*. How about human cloning and other ethical issues? Individual perspectives and visions should, at least, consider the ultimate limits. Frankl has strongly advocated that good and bad should be defined in terms of a meaningful existence.[148] The agility to define personal values is a great intellectual strength of a person, and an enlightened, precocious mind is capable of doing so. It is a purposeful human responsibility and failing which life can become chaotic and meaningless. By means of personal reasoning, such an insight of a responsible behavior can be found (it may be hard to develop through external manipulation). Even Frankl has suggested that values such as truth, beauty, and goodness need to be experienced alone.[149] No doubt, we are conditioned by the societal traditions, yet in our own individual way we are not a complete prototypical replicas of social establishments. In order to achieve higher order living each person, in the end, will have to triumph over self-serving intentions and values and thus facilitate a meaningful existence. On the contrary, uninhibited ideas will vilify the quality of human thinking and could lead to self-reduction. Human history have enough examples to prove that once the villainy prevails the results can be very destructive and uncivil. The recent pulsating rage of an American high school youth and his fatal shootings of his classmates in

---

[148] Viktor E. Frankl, *The Will to Meaning: Foundations and Applications of Logotherapy* (New York: The World Publishing Company, 1969), p. 68.

[149] Viktor E. Frankl, *The Doctor and the Soul: From Psychotherapy to Logotherapy* (New York: Alfred A. Knopf, Inc., 1965), p. 91.

Kentucky clearly represents the rampage of a disturbed mind. The current upsurge of violence among the youth in the United States is very heartbreaking and saddening. Such extremes of resentment among the young obviously has an underpinning of an existential vacuum and Frankl has strongly referred to this deficiency in his writings. This cascading turmoil among the youth is mind boggling, but a possible choice to soften this recalcitrant and wanton energy is to encourage the young mind to develop a value system of their own which is rational and purposeful. In the long range, intellectual and academic growth is expected to accomplish this goal in life. Periodically we need to evaluate our educational programs and determine if they are accomplishing these objectives. In view of this, my advance assessment is dismaying (the Juvenile and FBI Crime Reports further confirm this disappointing observation). Aggression among the young is one of the major social concerns, and how about drug addiction and the respect for law and order? Etiological assessment and explanation of these issues is a complex task.

If we look at the wide social spectrum, it is not too difficult to notice that the genuine happiness in life appears to be missing. People in the United States by large have the provision for the basic necessities but existence in itself is somewhat ruffled. Even the close relationships are to some extent volatile and at times bound by contractual agreements. Are we becoming less trustworthy or more quantitative in our mutual bond? Is individual profit the meaning of genuine love? These directions do not correspond to traditional values and may block to ensue the highest meaning of love. In my judgment love is not a demand; instead, it is a commitment to make each other's life more meaningful through an open and honest dialogue, with least feeling of censorship. In recent history Mother Teresa has shown us the ultimate meaning of love — a love without boundaries. Mother Teresa gave meaning to those destitute human beings whose lives had crumbled on the streets of Calcutta and had accepted that living in misery was the destiny of their existence. She cared for the poor and gave them the love, dignity, and an understanding of self–reliance in life.

In this age two loving persons may not necessarily be compatible but they can always bridge the difference by their complimentary expressions. Individual difference in perceptions and opinions is an integral part of living but mutual respect is paramount. In a loving relationship we owe responsibility to each other for one's personal growth. It is not a demand but a rightful human obligation. As humans we all have the same needs to be loved, feel secure, and live under conditions which are equal and just. Thus the exercise of one's personal freedom should account for these metapsychological needs. Individual freedom can either exalt or succumb one's existence, and we have to be mindful of the choices we make. A right–minded person will not opt to violate human dignity or trespass other's individual domain. It is painful to remember when in March 1997, thirty–nine members of the Heaven's Gate cult sedated themselves to death in San Diego, California. They must have lost a purpose in living and inappropriately executed their individual freedom.

We all possess soft spots, beliefs, and perspectives of the world we live in and vehemently protect those visions, especially under fears of external penetration. However, paths of life are seldom linear, and the wrinkles, if any, can be smoothed when we begin to live purposefully. The purpose in life provides the matrix on which the human bond is established. Basic needs of existence have a place of their own but those are representative of a passing phase and soon dissipate into some higher demands and the emphasis shifts to more purposeful goals. Purpose in life serves as a catalyst to elevate one's existence to a much higher platform and has the potential to abate self–serving needs. Ups and downs are inescapable realities of life and a person cannot limit his or her vision of optimism by the adversities of living. Life is a challenge and the unfavorable circumstances could provide an opportunity to discover one's worth, however, such chances are highly subjective to individual attitudes, attributes, and evaluations. The kind of choices we make under adverse conditions eventually determine our personal worth. Frankl claims that in order to discover one's meaning of life a person, at times, may have to go through some degree of sufferings and it may be considered as an inclusive pathway to discover self–worth.[150] The word *meaning* to Frankl implies a challenge, and thus, he used his personal atrocities of the Nazi concentration camps as an anvil to test his own belief that human sufferings could serve as a means to the discovery of personal worth. Frankl is opposed to nihilism and believes that

---

[150] Viktor E. Frankl, *Man's Search For Meaning: Revised and Updated* (New York: Washington Square Press, 1984), p. 137.

life certainly has a meaning and each of us have a mission to accomplish. Life, to Frankl, is more than a process of simple combustion.[151] In his writings, Frankl has attempted to make human sufferings more meaningful by relating them to some worthwhile outcomes. Frankl has encouraged a person to dare the adversities of life and has suggested that one should not submit himself to be conquered by the miseries of living. He firmly believes that person is capable of rising above his conditions because self-transcendence is the essence of existence.[152] This tenet of logotherapy implies that existence is purposeful only if it is directed toward some objective goals, beyond one's self. Frankl prefers to see each individual confronting and entangling himself into the circumstances of living rather than withdrawing from them.

Frankl's *Logotherapy* is considered as a psychotherapeutic technique to deal with human problems, and thus, it assists in the healing of emotional and mental disorders of a person.[153] Logotherapy promotes encountering existential predicaments and enlarges a person's vision to face the problems of life and free himself from the shackles of helplessness. Frankl believes that logotherapy:

> ... is realistic in that it faces the tragic
> triad of human existence: pain,
> death, and guilt. Logotherapy may

---

[151] Joseph B. Fabry, *The Pursuit of Meaning: Logotherapy Applied to Life* (Boston: Beacon Press, 1968), p. 10.

[152] Viktor E. Frankl, *Psychotherapy and Existentialism: Selected Papers on Logotherapy* (New York: Washington Square Press, Inc., 1967), p. 82.

[153] Godfryd Kaczanowski, "Logotherapy - A New Psychotherapeutic Tool," *Psychosomatics*, VIII (May-June, 1967), 159.

justly be called optimistic, because it
shows the person how to transform
despair into triumph.[154]

One must not overlook the reality that the individual himself is the principal agent in determining
his future, and should not allow himself to become
the victim of human squabbles and rancors. To look
for an escape from the challenges of life may not be the
best decision, and also, it could possibly lead to compromising the search for one's self-worth. Sometimes
best individual decisions are made under most challenging conditions. Throughout his writings Frankl
has represented himself as a stalwart of courage over
sorrow and Matthew Scully has correctly presented
him (Frankl) in a recent article by quoting:

> Life has meaning to the last breath.
> No matter what our circumstances
> there are always opportunities for
> courage, for facing our fate without
> flinching.[155]

In my own life, since childhood, I have gone
through circumstances which have been extremely
bitter to stomach, and there were those moments
when living became very difficult but I never lost
sight of the inner courage and encountered the events
with fortitude. Emotionally I have been shattered at
times but have resisted medical prescriptions to

---

[154] Viktor E. Frankl, *The Will To Meaning: Foundations and Applications of Logotherapy* (New York: The World Publishing Company, 1969), p. ix.
[155] Matthew Scully, "Facing Our Fate Without Flinching," *The Wall Street Journal* (September 4, 1997), p. A10.

manage my living, the storms came and poured hard yet failed to erode me because life has always carried a purpose for me. Most importantly what has kept me afloat and sailing is my personal conviction in the institution of God and without His blessings life could have been much harder to cope with. Incidentally it reminds me of what Ernest Hemingway has stated in his writings that if a person is strong during broken conditions then the chance for his mending the damage certainly increases, and it did for me. Most often our marginal responses to the challenges of life tend to become our abhorrent foes. I have learned from Tolstoy's writings that "time and patience" are the apropos of healing, and such ideas do own my deepest veneration. Mother Teresa's strong personal commitment to spiritual beliefs and in the institution of God offered her an inner strength to serve the destitute and the diseased tirelessly, and her efforts in the end helped many human beings to find a meaningful living in several countries of the world. Meaningful lives are discovered by those who take life as a challenge and confront events with courage and high spirits.

Frankl has not prescribed any preventative pre-scriptions to immune humans from hardships or judgmental errors because he believes that there are no specific predetermined solutions to demanding life events. It is not the contention of his theory (Logotherapy) to feed human beings in advance with a set of information and then expect the anticipated safeguards to emerge. In his opinion it is the individual conscience that ultimately serves as the final judge in the selection of a choice to encounter life events.

The purpose of life cannot be found on the basis of logical deductions; instead, it is realized through most demanding life endeavors. Intellectual activities alone may not provide the individual with an opportunity to have a clear grasp of one's purpose for living, it is something more than mental stimulation. Frankl believes that through spiritual enlightenment a person is capable of gaining an insight into his specific purpose of existence. Even though we believe that the nature of the culture and the society in which one lives determines the direction of his or her future paths, however, a person surely does own the capacity to influence and direct the course of his future existence. Logotherapy consistently aims to preserve an individual's worth and dignity in the facilitation of one's future, and thus, helps to discover a meaningful existence. Life is full of pressing examinations and one should attempt them as they come, with determination and courage, with least concerns for the past failure. The past is over but do not let the future slip by. Like a surfer who always looks forwards and tries to ride high and does not allow the waves to succumb him when conditions are in a state of turmoil. When currents of life are in our favor we feel good but rough waters have testing joys of their own, these two scenarios could follow each other. The currency of events is not always predictable but one can choose to mobilize positive energies and attitudes to confront them. In essence, personal cognitive strategies do make a difference and our mental labels define the course of action to be taken to encounter life's demands. Individual attitudes and perceptions create future possibilities and lend to productive results. At times we get fettered and caged by our individual self-defeating mental paradigms and prematurely concede to failures and hence surrender the purpose of our existence.

As individuals, we do own and recognize our biological and psychological variations, yet at the core of our existence we have a high degree of sameness. Individually we possess an autonomy of the mind and are capable of making independent decisions, but spiritually we care for each other and attempt to seek peaceful solutions to our existential problems and challenges. Circumstances of living and environmental conditions do shape us to develop individual personality traits which represent distinction, however, at the center of our spiritual mind we are very much alike. Survival demands of the world may pressure us to be competitive in our behaviors but within the spiritual nexus we are almost identical in being helpful to each other, and highly desire to become worthy members of the human community. We fear insignificance and consider life to be meaningless when there is a lack of purpose in living. This deficit of a purpose in life creates an existential confusion and hence a spiritual hole. Frankl has carefully addressed this spiritual emptiness and has diagnosed it to be the principal cause of turmoil in our lives today. A lack of purpose in life lends to functional chaos and an existential void. Frankl envisions this as a universal human concern and throughout his writings has encouraged each person to make a concerted effort to discover this unique individual purpose of life. Having such an insight in life makes living meaningful and creative. Frankl has emphasized that, as humans, we need to have a purpose in life, that is, a personal commitment to some responsible goal and it should direct our thoughts and actions. Frankl has most appropriately delivered this message and as an intellectual has earned a global respect for his theoretical concepts and writings, which evolved from his personal life experiences of the World War II and professional medical practice.